DATE DUE

The Modern Language Association of America

Selected Bibliographies in Language and Literature

1. Roger D. Lund. *Restoration and Early Eighteenth-Century English Literature, 1660–1740: A Selected Bibliography of Resource Materials.* 1980.

2. Richard Kempton. *French Literature: An Annotated Guide to Selected Bibliographies.* 1981.

3. William A. Wortman. *A Guide to Serial Bibliographies for Modern Literatures.* 1982.

4. Hensley C. Woodbridge. *Spanish and Spanish-American Literature: An Annotated Guide to Selected Bibliographies.* 1983.

5. Hensley C. Woodbridge. *Guide to Reference Works for the Study of the Spanish Language and Literature and Spanish American Literature.* 1987.

6. Bobby J. Chamberlain. *Portuguese Language and Luso-Brazilian Literature: An Annotated Guide to Selected Reference Works.* 1989.

7. Laura Sue Fuderer. *The Female Bildungsroman in English: An Annotated Bibliography of Criticism.* 1990.

The Female Bildungsroman in English

An Annotated Bibliography of Criticism

Laura Sue Fuderer

The Modern Language Association of America
New York, NY   1990

Copyright © 1990 by The Modern Language Association of America

Library of Congress Cataloging-in-Publication Data

Fuderer, Laura Sue, 1944–
    The female bildungsroman in English: an annotated bibliography of
criticism / Laura Sue Fuderer.
      p.   cm.
    Includes index.
    ISBN 0-87352-962-6 (P)
    1. English fiction—Women authors—History and criticism—
Bibliography. 2. American fiction—Women authors—History and
criticism—Bibliography. 3. Women and literature—Bibliography.
4. Women in literature—Bibliography. 5. Bildungsroman—
Bibliography. I. Title.
Z2013.5.W6F83   1990
[PR830.W6]
016.823009'9287—dc20   90-39517

Published by The Modern Language Association of America
10 Astor Place, New York, New York 10003-6981

Contents

Introduction *1*

Books *8*

Articles in Books *14*

Articles in Periodicals *19*

Abstracts in *Dissertation Abstracts International* (*DAI*) *31*

Female Bildungsromane *34*

Index *44*

Introduction

Until the rise of feminist criticism the bildungsroman was tradition-
ally regarded as the novel of the development of a young man in the
style of Goethe's *Wilhelm Meister*. During the 1970s feminist critics began to identify a new or at least revised genre, the female bildungsroman,
the novel of the development of a female protagonist. This selected bibliography is an initial effort to list books, articles, and dissertations about
such novels written in English by women authors. It also lists over 250
novels identified in the criticism.

Because much of the critical literature attempts to redefine an existing genre, the question of definition arises. Frequently cited works that
contribute to a definition of the English tradition of the bildungsroman
include Susanne Howe's *Wilhelm Meister and His English Kinsmen: Apprentices to Life*, Maurice Beebe's *Ivory Towers and Sacred Founts: The
Artist Hero in Fiction from Goethe to Joyce*, and Jerome Buckley's *Season of Youth: The Bildungsroman from Dickens to Golding*. Buckley's
"broadest outline" of the plot is the following:

A child of some sensibility grows up in the country or in a provincial
town, where he finds constraints, social and intellectual, placed upon the
free imagination. His family, especially his father, proves doggedly hostile to his creative instincts or flights of fancy, antagonistic to his ambi-
tions, and quite impervious to the new ideas he has gained from
unprescribed reading. His first schooling, even if not totally inadequate,
may be frustrating insofar as it may suggest options not available to him
in his present setting. He therefore, sometimes at quite an early age, leaves
the repressive atmosphere of home (and also the relative innocence), to
make his way independently in the city (in the English novels, usually
London). There his real "education" begins, not only his preparation for
a career but also—and often more importantly—his direct experience of
urban life. The latter involves at least two love affairs or sexual encoun-

ters, one debasing, one exalting, and demands that in this respect and others the hero reappraise his values. (18)

C. Hugh Holman's definition in his *Handbook to Literature* is also frequently cited. He refers to the bildungsroman as the apprenticeship novel and describes it as:

> A NOVEL which recounts the youth and young manhood of a sensitive PROTAGONIST who is attempting to learn the nature of the world, discover its meaning and pattern, and acquire a philosophy of life and "the art of living." (39)

All these works except Holman's cite at least one novel by a woman author among their examples, and Beebe identifies Mme de Staël's *Corinne* as the model of the art novel, or *Künstlerroman*. But they tend to conceive of the genre as a male form, and most of their exemplars are by men.

Discussions of the female bildungsroman began to appear in the critical literature in the early 1970s, when critics recognized its rise as a reflection of the contemporary feminist movement. One of the earliest, a 1972 article by Ellen Morgan, identifies the female bildungsroman as a "recasting" of an old form that was distinctly male until the twentieth century. She describes the genre as "the most salient form for literature influenced by neo-feminism" because "[w]oman as neo-feminism conceives of her is a creature in the process of becoming, struggling to throw off her conditioning, the psychology of oppression" (183–85). In an article written in 1979 Bonnie Hoover Braendlin cites Morgan's concept of a revision of an old form and adds:

> . . . the feminist bildungsroman delineates woman's self-development toward a viable present and future existence, free from predetermined, male-dominated societal roles, which in the past have yielded a fragmented rather than a satisfactorily integrated personality. (18)

Barbara Anne White contrasts the novel of adolescence with the bildungsroman in her book *Growing Up Female*, published in 1985. Distinguishing between the two forms, she comments, "whatever the reason for the older protagonist's success, the fact that she moves toward achieving 'authentic female selfhood' makes the modern feminist *Bildungsroman* the most popular form of feminist fiction" (195). Two other critics, writing in 1986, point out the correlation between the literary genre and changing social conditions. In *The Myth of the Heroine* Esther Kleinbord Labovitz terms the female bildungsroman a twentieth-century genre "made possible only when *Bildung* became a reality for women" (6–7). In a fine theoretical analysis of the novel of self-discovery, Rita Felski states categorically, "The increasing visibility of the novel of self-discovery is obviously related to the growth of feminism as a contemporary ideology and to the changing social and economic status of women" (131). She continues, "[T]he *Bildungsroman* may well be acquiring a new function as an articulation of women's new sense of identity and increasing movement into public life" (137).

Not all critics have been so optimistic regarding the success or even the possibility of *Bildung* for women protagonists. Most of them qualify the sort of self-realization achieved by women. The optimism sensed by Felski lies in escape from entrapment and assertion of "a separate identity beyond the male sphere" (132). Frequent reference is made to an excerpt from *The Madwoman in the Attic*, in which Sandra M. Gilbert and Susan Gubar, referring to *Jane Eyre*, delineate the difficulties faced by the protagonist of the female bildungsroman:

> [It is] a story of enclosure and escape, a distinctively female Bildungsro-
> man in which the problems encountered by the protagonist as she strug-
> gles from the imprisonment of her childhood toward an almost
> unthinkable goal of mature freedom are symptomatic of difficulties Every-
> woman in a patriarchal society must meet and overcome: oppression (at
> Gateshead), starvation (at Lowood), madness (at Thornfield), and cold-
> ness (at Marsh End). . . . (338–39)

In the article cited above, Braendlin observes:

> The modern feminist bildungsroman usually depicts adolescent develop-
> ment to one extent or another, but it focuses primarily upon the crisis
> occasioned by a woman's awakening, in her late twenties or early thir-
> ties, to the stultification and fragmentation of a personality devoted not
> to self-fulfillment and awareness, but to a culturally determined, self-
> sacrificing, and self-effacing existence. This crisis and the resultant struggle
> for individuality and integration continue to occupy the central thematic
> position of the feminist bildungsroman in the mid-seventies. (18)

Annis Pratt and Barbara White's chapter on the novel of development in *Archetypal Patterns in Women's Fiction* describes early female coming-of-age novels as providing models for "growing down" rather than "growing up" (14). In her 1987 book about the fiction of Jean Stafford, Maureen Ryan writes:

> The female *Bildungsroman*, then, is traditionally a tale of compromise
> and disillusionment, the chronicle of a young woman's recognition that,

for her, life offers not limitless possibilities but an unsympathetic environment in which she must struggle to discover a room of her own.   (14–15)

Some critics observe that, if individual development and integration into the community have appeared difficult for the female protagonist, the obstacles are greatly compounded when that protagonist faces racial prejudice in addition to restrictive gender roles. In an article published in 1982 Sondra O'Neale contrasts the bildungsroman themes by selected black American women writers with those of the traditional Western male-oriented bildungsroman. She observes:

> [They] collectively depict the Black woman's internal struggle to unravel the immense complexities of racial identity, gender definitions (in contexts of Black and not white experience), and awakening of sexual being— in short to discover, direct, and recreate the self in the midst of hostile racial, sexual and other societal repression—to produce a literature not confined to 'usual' *Bildung* development at set chronological ages.   (25)

Instead of proposing a variant or revision of an existing tradition, O'Neale protests the appropriation of the genre as "measured only by the testimony of a select group of men." She sees the character development in the black female bildungsroman as the inverse of that in the male form in four ways: (1) the protagonist's "ripeness" for the process occurs at an older age; (2) she must relinquish the hope for assimilation into black spheres in order to attain "discovery, growth and wisdom"; (3) she has no mentors to assist her; and (4) once the struggle is over she has no "tribe"—no "supportive community initiators"—to join (25–27). Writing a year later in an article titled "*Bildung* in Ethnic Women Writers," Braendlin similarly recognizes a new bildungsroman being written by "disenfranchised Americans—women, Blacks, Mexican-Americans, native Americans, homosexuals" and evincing "a revaluation, a transvaluation, of traditional *Bildung* by new standards and perspectives" (75).

In a 1979 article titled "The Novel of Awakening," Susan J. Rosowski identifies the awakening novel as the female counterpart to the male bildungsroman. She sees a difference, however: unlike the bildungsroman with its outward movement toward self-fulfillment through integration into society, the awakening novel is characterized by an inward movement toward greater self-knowledge and the realization that the art of living is difficult or impossible for a woman. Rosowski calls this development "an awakening to limitations" (313). Elaine Martin, in a theoretical construct based on an analysis of French and German novels, also favors the novel of awakening as the female alternative to the bildungsroman. She questions Morgan's optimism about the bildungs-roman as "a vehicle to express change" and hypothesizes that "in novels with a female hero, a linear quest means confrontation with society, and that in turn means 'defeat'. . . ." She thus distinguishes between the bildungsroman-apprenticeship novel, which is a linear and a male form, and the initiation-awakening model, which is vertical and female (51–52).

Other critics have considered the female bildungsroman a contradiction in terms and have suggested alternative or variant forms. Elaine Hoffman Baruch, writing in 1981, states, "The authentic feminine *bildungsroman* remains to be written." Because the heroine's development is inextricably linked to marriage and because marriage invariably restricts women, she calls the novels "bildungsromans manqués" (357). In the article cited above, Pratt and White make the following observation:

> In the woman's novel of development (exclusive of the science fiction genre), however, the hero does not *choose* a life to one side of society after conscious deliberation on the subject; rather, she is radically alienated by gender-role norms *from the very outset*. Thus, although the authors attempt to accommodate their hero's *Bildung*, or development, to the general pattern of the genre, the disjunctions that we have noted inevitably make the woman's initiation less a self-determined progression *towards* maturity than a regression *from* full participation in adult life. It seems more appropriate to use the term *Entwicklungsroman*, the novel of mere growth, mere physical passage from one age to the other without psychological development, to describe most of the novels that we have perused. (36)

In her 1985 article Barbara Frey Waxman coins the term *Reifungsroman* to identify a subgenre of the bildungsroman and to distinguish the "growing up" of the middle-aged protagonist from the "growing down" of the youthful heroine in the typical female bildungsroman (320–21).

The bibliography that follows cites books, articles in books and in periodicals, and dissertations that deal either with the genre of the female bildungsroman or with novels described as such. Also included are works about the novel of awakening or of self-discovery more generally that shed light on the female bildungsroman. The bibliography covers works published primarily from 1972 to 1987 with a few exceptions, such as Howe (1930), Beebe (1964), and other major studies of the traditional bildungsroman that discuss novels by women. Reprints are identified where possible to enhance availability of sources through smaller institutions. Criticism on specific titles is restricted to studies of novels by women. Thus articles are excluded if they discuss female bildungsromane written by men, such as Flaubert's *Madame Bovary* and Hardy's *Tess of the d'Urbervilles*, and other genres such as short stories and poems, such as Elizabeth Barrett Browning's *Aurora Leigh.*

The brief annotations are intended to convey the significance of each work to the generic study of the bildungsroman. They also identify the specific works of fiction that are evaluated or cited as exemplars. For the dissertations a reference is given to *Dissertation Abstracts International (DAI)* in place of an annotation. The final section of the bibliography is a list of the novels cited in the criticism.

A review of the issues raised by the criticism listed in this bibliography suggests several directions for future exploration. An obvious one is a supplement that identifies studies of the female bildungsroman or, more inclusively, the female novel of self-discovery in literatures of the non-English-speaking world. More cross-cultural comparisons like Rita Felski's would enlighten the theoretical debate. She regards the novel of self-discovery as the literary reflection of neofeminism but notes cultural distinctions. Felski considers the bildungsroman model as more typical of the United States, where there is a broad-based support of feminism, and the awakening novel as more prevalent in West Germany, where feminism has achieved a marginal position, and in Canada, where emancipation is linked with "the experience of the wilderness" (139–40). Felski's distinction both supports and qualifies Martin's conclusion that the novel of awakening, not the bildungsroman, is the authentic female genre. Both critics suggest the importance of social, economic, and political differences among cultures, and further elaboration of the correlation between these factors and literary form is in order.

The theoretical debate continues on whether the female bildungsroman as a genre is a revision, a variant, a subgenre, an expansion, or an impossibility. Related lines of inquiry deal with the female bildungsroman by male writers and vice versa, the so-called double bildungsroman (e.g., the parallel development of brother and sister), and the bildungsroman of a middle-aged protagonist and include the respective places of these forms in the theoretical framework of the genre.

Finally, as several critics assure us, female novels of self-discovery and development are alive and well in the late 1980s. Each new novel offers an opportunity for study in relation to past criticism and to the ongoing debate on the female bildungsroman.

Works Cited

Baruch, Elaine Hoffman. "The Feminine Bildungsroman: Education through Marriage." *Massachusetts Review* 22 (1981): 335–57.

Beebe, Maurice. *Ivory Towers and Sacred Founts: The Artist Hero in Fiction from Goethe to Joyce.* New York: New York State UP, 1964.

Braendlin, Bonnie Hoover. "Alther, Atwood, Ballantyne, and Gray: Secular Salvation in the Contemporary Feminist Bildungsroman." *Frontiers: A Journal of Women Studies* 4.1 (1979): 18–22.

——. "*Bildung* in Ethnic Women Writers." *Denver Quarterly* 17 (1983): 75–87.

Buckley, Jerome. *Season of Youth: The Bildungsroman from Dickens to Golding.* Cambridge: Harvard UP, 1974.

Felski, Rita. "The Novel of Self-Discovery: A Necessary Fiction?" *Southern Review* 19 (1986): 131–48.

Gilbert, Sandra M., and Susan Gubar. *The Madwoman in the Attic: The Woman Writer and the Nineteenth-Century Literary Imagination.* New Haven: Yale UP, 1979.

Holman, C. Hugh. *A Handbook to Literature.* 3rd ed. Indianapolis: Odyssey, 1972.

Howe, Susanne. *Wilhelm Meister and His English Kinsmen: Apprentices to Life.* New York: Columbia UP, 1930; AMS, 1966.

Labovitz, Esther Kleinbord. *The Myth of the Heroine: The Female* Bildungsroman *in the Twentieth Century: Dorothy Richardson, Simone de Beauvoir, Doris Lessing, Christa Wolf.* New York: Lang, 1986.

Martin, Elaine. "Theoretical Soundings: The Female Archetypal Quest in Contemporary French and German Women's Fiction." *Perspectives on Contemporary Literature* 8 (1983): 48–57.

Morgan, Ellen. "Humanbecoming: Form and Focus in the Neo-Feminist Novel." *Images of Women in Fiction: Feminist Perspectives.* Ed. Susan Koppelman Cornillon. Bowling Green: Bowling Green U Popular P, 1972. 183–205.

O'Neale, Sondra. "Race, Sex and Self: Aspects of Bildung in Select Novels by Black American Women Novelists." *MELUS: The Journal of the Society for the Study of the Multi-Ethnic Literature of the United States* 9.4 (1982): 25–37.

Pratt, Annis, and Barbara White. "The Novel of Development." *Archetypal Patterns in Women's Fiction.* Bloomington: Indiana UP, 1981. 13–37.

Rosowski, Susan J. "The Novel of Awakening." *Genre* 12 (1979): 313–32.

Ryan, Maureen. *Innocence and Estrangement in the Fiction of Jean Stafford.* Baton Rouge: Louisiana State UP, 1987.

Waxman, Barbara Frey. "From *Bildungsroman* to *Reifungsroman*: Aging in Doris Lessing's Fiction." *Soundings: An Interdisciplinary Journal* 68 (1985): 318–34.

White, Barbara Anne. *Growing Up Female: Adolescent Girlhood in American Fiction.* Westport: Greenwood, 1985.

Books

⟩ 1.   Abel, Elizabeth, Marianne Hirsch, and Elizabeth Langland, eds. *The Voyage In: Fictions of Female Development*. Hanover: UP of New England for Dartmouth Coll., 1983.

In "Spiritual *Bildung*: The Beautiful Soul as Paradigm" Marianne Hirsch takes a psychoanalytic approach to contrast the male with the female bildungsroman. Identifies Goethe's *Wilhelm Meister* as containing the paradigm for both and as revealing the female version to be circular, inward-directed, and reflective of a preoedipal psychological phase that is the basis of female personality. Analyzes George Eliot's *Mill on the Floss*, Theodor Fontane's *Effi Briest*, and Kate Chopin's *Awakening*. (For Susan Rosowski's "Novel of Awakening" see "Articles in Periodicals" below.) In "'Fairy-born and human-bred': Jane Eyre's Education in Romance" Karen E. Rowe sees the female bildungsroman as strongly influenced by the romantic fairy tale with its limited female maturation. Uses Charlotte Brontë's *Jane Eyre* as an example that partially conforms to Jerome Buckley's definition of the traditional bildungsroman but that is related far more to the fairy-tale subgenre. In "The Reflecting Reader in *Villette*" Brenda R. Silver suggests that the narrator, Lucy Snowe, by absorbing the reader into her text, creates a community that will accept her nontraditional development, which is unacceptable to the community in the novel. In "Female Stories of Experience: Alcott's *Little Women* in Light of *Work*" Elizabeth Langland sees *Work* as expressing an alternative life-style to that in *Little Women*. Considers the former as offering fulfillment in the context of female community instead of marriage to one man and as contradicting traditional feminine qualities of passivity and self-suppression. In "The Sisterhood of Jane Eyre and Antoinette Cosway" Elizabeth R. Baer describes Jean Rhys's *Wide Sargasso Sea* as both revision and preview of Brontë's *Jane Eyre*, and sees the two protagonists as parallel victims of patriarchy whose lives merge in a mutual act of survival. (For Blanche H. Gelfant's "Revolutionary Turnings: *The Mountain Lion* Reread" see "Articles in Periodicals.") In "Narrative Structure(s) and Female Development: The Case of *Mrs. Dalloway*" Elizabeth Abel analyzes Virginia Woolf's work as a subversive interplay of gender and genre in which varying levels of text and plot, of silence and revelation, are used to convey female development, "a story of preoedipal attachment and loss." In "Doris Lessing and the Parables of Growth"

Catharine R. Stimpson considers the whole five-volume *Children of Violence* series a bildungsroman. Suggests Lessing has revised the genre to reflect the development of an individual's "power of consciousness" and has enlarged it to incorporate "Western apocalyptic tradition" with its setting in the tumultuous twentieth century. In "Through the Looking Glass: When Women Tell Fairy Tales" Ellen Cronan Rose views the fairy tale as the paradigmatic story of female development (and limitation) and gauges its influence on Anne Sexton's *Transformations*, Olga Broumas's *Beginning with O*, and Angela Carter's "Bloody Chamber." (For Mary Anne Ferguson's "Female Novel of Development and the Myth of Psyche" see "Articles in Periodicals.") In "Exiting from Patriarchy: The Lesbian Novel of Development" Bonnie Zimmerman describes the lesbian novel of development as resembling the classic bildungsroman more than it does the feminist novel of awakening. Refers to numerous examples but discusses at greater length Christa Winsloe's *Child Manuela* and June Arnold's *Sister Gin*. In "'Why are you afraid to have me at your side?': From Passivity to Power in *Salt of the Earth*" Margo Kasdan analyzes the development of the female protagonist in this movie by blacklisted Hollywood directors. In "Plain, Black, and Decently Wild: The Heroic Possibilities of *Maud Martha*" Mary Helen Washington views Gwendolyn Brooks's autobiographical novel as an attempt to confront the silence forced on black women and to break it by using a protagonist who voices "a rare self-awareness." In "*Family Ties*: Female Development in Clarice Lispector" Marta Peixoto aims to amend critical neglect of the female dimension of Lispector's characters by discussing the self-awareness, initiation, or growth of the female protagonists in this short-story collection. In "Shadowing/Surfacing/Shedding: Contemporary German Writers in Search of a Female *Bildungsroman*" Sandra Frieden observes that German female development novels of the 1970s reveal a distinctive female bildungsroman that has evolved from the traditional male bildungsroman, a postwar blurring of the distinction between autobiographical fiction and nonfiction, and the explorations of new roles for women in society. Applies the concept to Ingeborg Bachmann's *Malina*, Brigitte Schwaiger's *Wie kommt das Salz ins Meer?* and Verena Stefan's *Häutungen*.

2.   Baym, Nina. *Woman's Fiction: A Guide to Novels by and about Women in America, 1820–1870*. Ithaca: Cornell UP, 1978.

Resurrects popular women writers neglected by later arbiters of the literary canon and tries to identify their enormous appeal for nineteenth-century American readers. Sees in the works the common tale of a heroine unprepared for adversity but forced into developing self-reliance in order to triumph. Does not use the term *bildungsroman* but describes the plot as "the story of the formation and assertion of a feminine ego." Chapters feature Catharine Sedgwick, Maria McIntosh, E. D. E. N. Southworth, Caroline Lee Hentz, Susan Warner, Anna Warner, Maria Cummins, Ann Sophia Stephens, Mary Jane Holmes, Marion Harland, Caroline Chesebro', and Augusta Jane Evans but also discuss others.

✗ 3.   Christ, Carol P. *Diving Deep and Surfacing: Women Writers on Spiritual Quest*. Boston: Beacon, 1980.

Equates contemporary woman's discovery of the need for self-affirmation with a quest for spiritual grounding, a quest that proceeds from nothingness to awakening to insight to "new naming," although the movement is not always that linear. Echoes Annis Pratt on the need for a myth of the heroine and a female bildungsroman that parallel the male versions. Elucidates the spiritual quest in Kate Chopin's *Awakening*, Margaret Atwood's *Surfacing*, Doris Lessing's *Children of Violence* series, and poetry by Adrienne Rich and Ntozake Shange.

4.   Dalsimer, Katherine. *Female Adolescence: Psychoanalytic Reflections on Works of Literature*. New Haven: Yale UP, 1986.

Uses a psychoanalytical approach to shed light on stories of female adolescence, "the experience of the girl in becoming a woman." Suggests that recent developments in psychoanalytic theory have enhanced understanding of the female experience, long considered distinctive from the male but inadequately understood. Chapters consider Carson McCullers's *Member of the Wedding*, Muriel Spark's *Prime of Miss Jean Brodie*, Jane Austen's *Persuasion*, *The Diary of Ann Frank*, and *Romeo and Juliet*.

5.   Edwards, Lee R. *Psyche as Hero: Female Heroism and Fictional Form*. Middletown: Wesleyan UP, 1984.

Takes an approach that relates to the study of the female bildungsroman but does not refer to it as such. Considers "Western culture's opposing self," the woman hero who applies feminine rather than masculine qualities to confront society and seek change. Sees in the myth of Psyche the pattern of the growth of consciousness pertaining to human, not just female or male, development and change. Evaluates in these terms the female hero in works by both men and women, including Charlotte Brontë's *Jane Eyre*, George Eliot's *Middlemarch*, Kate Chopin's *Awakening*, Agnes Smedley's *Daughter of Earth*, Dorothy Sayers's *Gaudy Night*, Toni Morrison's *Sula*, Zora Neale Hurston's *Their Eyes Were Watching God*, Harriette Arnow's *Dollmaker*, Maxine Hong Kingston's *Woman Warrior*, Virginia Woolf's *Mrs. Dalloway*, and Doris Lessing's *Memoirs of a Survivor*.

✗ 6.   Frye, Joanne S. *Living Stories, Telling Lives: Women and the Novel in Contemporary Experience*. Ann Arbor: U of Michigan P, 1986.

Observes that the male protagonist of the bildungsroman affirms his manhood and his autonomy while the female is forced to choose between the mothering-feminine role and "individuation." Explores the difficulties women authors have in creating protagonists who are both autonomous and female and considers the reasons these authors frequently use the first-person narrative. Examines Alice Munro's *Lives of Girls and Women* and Toni Morrison's *Bluest Eye* particularly as bildungsromane, and also Gail Godwin's *Violet Clay*, Margaret Laurence's *Stone Angel*, Margaret Drabble's *Waterfall*, and Doris Lessing's *Golden Notebook*.

✕ 7.   Gullette, Margaret Morganroth. *Safe at Last in the Middle Years: The Invention of the Midlife Progress Novel: Saul Bellow, Margaret Drabble, Anne Tyler, and John Updike*. Berkeley: U of California P, 1988.

Presenting the midlife progress novel as a genre belying the commonplace that life declines with age, Gullette examines protagonists who progress toward meaning, serenity, fulfillment, freedom, or some other goal. Expresses uncertainty about the name for this genre and observes that some identify it with the bildungsroman. Devotes most of chapter 4 to Drabble's *Jerusalem the Golden* and notes that the bildungsroman "was and is her literary form." In another chapter Gullette surveys eight of Anne Tyler's novels, from *The Clock Winder* to *The Accidental Tourist*.

8.   Huf, Linda. *A Portrait of the Artist as a Young Woman: The Writer as Heroine in American Literature*. New York: Ungar, 1983.

Contends that the female *Künstlerroman* differs substantially from the male both in the protagonist's character and in her "ruling conflict." Suggests that the woman artist feels guilty and selfish for pursuing her art, as evidenced by common images of monsters, entrapment, and attempted flight in the novels. Separate chapters discuss Fanny Fern's *Ruth Hall*, Elizabeth Stuart Phelps Ward's *Story of Avis*, Kate Chopin's *Awakening*, Willa Cather's *Song of the Lark*, Carson McCullers's *Heart Is a Lonely Hunter*, and Sylvia Plath's *Bell Jar*.

9.   Jones, Anne Goodwyn. *Tomorrow Is Another Day: The Woman Writer in the South, 1859–1936*. Baton Rouge: Louisiana State UP, 1981.

Includes chapters on several writers and specifically discusses as bildungsromane Augusta Jane Evans's *Beulah*, Kate Chopin's *Awakening*, Margaret Mitchell's *Gone with the Wind*, and Mary Johnston's *Hagar*.

10.   Labovitz, Esther Kleinbord. *The Myth of the Heroine. The Female Bildungsroman in the Twentieth Century: Dorothy Richardson, Simone de Beauvoir, Doris Lessing, Christa Wolf*. New York: Lang, 1987.

Finds no female bildungsroman in nineteenth-century literature because "this new genre was made possible only when *Bildung* became a reality for women." Proposes to examine the cultural and thematic implications of the bildungsroman for the female protagonist and simultaneously to "discover the rationale for her exclusion from its history." Selects four authors whose works best illustrate the new genre and devotes chapters to Dorothy Miller Richardson's *Pilgrimage*, Simone de Beauvoir's *Memoirs of a Dutiful Daughter*, Doris Lessing's *Children of Violence*, and Christa Wolf's *Quest for Christa T*.

11.   Moretti, Franco. *The Way of the World: The Bildungsroman in European Culture*. London: Verso, 1987.

Traces the tradition of the European bildungsroman from its aesthetic and archetypal models to the divergence between the Continental and the English types. Makes no distinctions between the male and female experience, and Jane Austen's *Pride and Prejudice* and Goethe's *Wilhelm Meister* are regarded and cited equally as archetypes. Discusses Charlotte Brontë's *Jane Eyre* and George Eliot's *Middlemarch* among other bildungsromane.

12.   Pearson, Carol, and Katherine Pope. *The Female Hero in American and British Literature.* New York: Bowker, 1981.

Rejecting the term *heroine*, revises the hero myth to include literary works about female protagonists who display heroic qualities as they embark on journeys of self-discovery. Refers to over two hundred works by both men and women since early 1800, describing some, including those by Erica Jong and Charlotte Brontë, as belonging to a new form of bildungsroman that "combines literary elements with essayistic ones."

13.   Rose, Ellen Cronan. *The Tree outside the Window: Doris Lessing's* Children of Violence. Hanover: UP of New England, 1976.

Applies Eriksonian "egopsychology" to Lessing's series of novels because Erikson's concern, like that of the bildungsroman, is for both the development of the individual and the individual's relation to society. Questions whether Lessing's heroine, Martha Quest, achieved a sense of identity while coming to terms with society as did Goethe's hero, Wilhelm Meister, in the prototype of the genre. Rose concludes that *Children of Violence* constitutes a problematic but genuine bildungsroman—one that changes the question from whether the individual can achieve a sense of identity in a hostile society to what sort of identity can be achieved in such a society.

14.   Ryan, Maureen. *Innocence and Estrangement in the Fiction of Jean Stafford.* Baton Rouge: Louisiana State UP, 1987.

Using a feminist perspective, Ryan considers Stafford's fiction with theoretical reference to Annis Pratt's *Archetypal Patterns in Women's Fiction*, especially Pratt's conception of the novel of development. Ryan views the female experience of development as one of submission to societal forces rather than of integration into society. With frequent reference to the female bildungsroman, she discusses Jean Stafford's *Boston Adventure, The Mountain Lion, The Catherine Wheel*, and the short stories.

15.   Stewart, Grace. *A New Mythos: The Novel of the Artist as Heroine, 1877–1977.* St. Albans: Eden, 1979.

Questions the universality of the mythic pattern of the artist as hero (as opposed to heroine) and analyzes eighteen female *Künstlerromane* to identify distinctively female myths. The novels are by Margaret Atwood, Mary Hunter Austin, Esther M. Broner, Willa Cather, Zelda Fitzgerald, Pamela Hansford Johnson, Erica Jong, Doris Lessing, Natalie L. M. Petesch, Sylvia Plath, Dorothy Miller Richardson, May Sarton, May Sinclair, Muriel Spark, Elizabeth Stuart Phelps Ward, and Virginia Woolf.

16.　White, Barbara Anne. *Growing Up Female: Adolescent Girlhood in American Fiction*. Westport: Greenwood, 1985.

In defining the female novel of adolescence, White distinguishes it from the bildungsroman. Observes that in the former the protagonist is younger, more sheltered from disillusionment, and less likely to question traditional values. The adolescent heroine exhibits neither the growth in knowledge nor the development in character experienced by the heroine of the bildungsroman; and the genre is "characterized by conflict relating to the low status of adolescence." Chapters cover Edith Wharton's *Summer*, Ruth Suckow's fiction, Carson McCullers's *Member of the Wedding*, and Jean Stafford's *Mountain Lion*.

Articles in Books

17.   Adams, Marianne. "*Jane Eyre*: Woman's Estate." *The Authority of Experience: Essays in Feminist Criticism*. Ed. Arlyn Diamond and Lee R. Edwards. Amherst: U of Massachusetts P, 1977. 137–59.

Identifies Charlotte Brontë's novel as a female bildungsroman and traces Jane's development in the face of her conflicting needs for love and independence.

18.   Beebe, Maurice. "Art As Experience: The Sacred Fount Tradition." *Ivory Towers and Sacred Founts: The Artist as Hero in Fiction from Goethe to Joyce*. New York: New York UP, 1964. 65–113.

Identifies the artist-novel as a type of bildungsroman and cites Susanne Howe's distinction between the apprentice who adjusts to the environment and the artist who remains apart from it. Discusses as *Künstlerromane* Mme de Staël's *Corinne*, George Sand's *Consuelo*, and Geraldine Jewsbury's *Half Sisters*. Observes that, for women protagonists, when art "conflicts with one's duty as wife and mother, it must be sacrificed."

19.   Buckley, Jerome. "George Eliot: A Double Life." *Season of Youth: The Bildungsroman from Dickens to Golding*. Cambridge: Harvard UP, 1974. 92–115. Rpt. in *From Smollett to James: Studies in the Novel and Other Essays Presented to Edgar Johnson*. Ed. Samuel I. Mintz, Alice Chandler, and Christopher Mulvey. Charlottesville: UP of Virginia, 1981. 211–36.

Analyzes the autobiographical elements of *The Mill on the Floss*, among other representative Victorian bildungsromane in which "each writer in turn learned to accommodate a powerful personal vision to the developing conventions of the genre."

20.   Chase, Karen. "Where Is Jane Eyre?" *Eros and Psyche: The Representation of Personality in Charlotte Brontë, Charles Dickens, and George Eliot*. New York: Methuen, 1984. 66–91.

Discusses conflicts and syntheses "between love and self, romance and Bildung" in Charlotte Brontë's *Jane Eyre*, *Villette*, and *Shirley*.

21. Christian, Barbara. "Trajectories of Self-Definition: Placing Contemporary Afro-American Women's Fiction." *Black Feminist Criticism: Perspectives on Black Women Writers*. New York: Pergamon, 1985. 171–86. Also in *Conjuring: Black Women, Fiction and Literary Tradition*. Ed. Hortense J. Spillers and Marjorie Pryse. Bloomington: Indiana UP, 1985. 233–48.

Traces the theme of self-definition of the heroine (without using the term *bildungsroman*) in numerous Afro-American bildungsromane from Frances E. W. Harper's *Iola LeRoy* to Paule Marshall's *Praisesong for the Widow*.

22. DuPlessis, Rachel Blau. "To Bear My Mother's Name: Künstlerromane by Women Writers." *Writing beyond the Ending: Narrative Strategies of Twentieth-Century Women Writers*. Bloomington: Indiana UP, 1985. 84–104.

Proposes that the twentieth-century writer's solution to the conflict between domestic and artistic choices faced by the *Künstlerroman* heroine lies in the daughter's fulfilling the mother's thwarted talents. Considers Elizabeth Barrett Browning's *Aurora Leigh*, Virginia Woolf's *To the Lighthouse*, Margaret Atwood's *Surfacing*, Doris Lessing's *Golden Notebook*, and others.

23. Gardner, Susan, and Carole Ferrier. "*My Brilliant Career*: Portrait of the Artist as a Wild Colonial Girl." *Gender, Politics, and Fiction: Twentieth Century Australian Women's Novels*. Ed. Carole Ferrier. St. Lucia: U of Queensland P, 1985. 22–43.

Rereads Miles Franklin's novel in terms of Annis Pratt's nonlinear "green world" archetype and attributes its enduring appeal to "a particularly female fictional pattern" rendered in a colonial context.

24. Goodman, Charlotte. "Women Novelists and the Male-Female Double Bildungsroman." *Transformations in Literature and Film: Selected Papers from the Sixth Annual Florida State University Conference on Literature and Film*. Ed. Leon Golden. Tallahassee: UP of Florida, 1982. 9–16. Expanded in "The Lost Brother, the Twin: Women Novelists and the Male-Female Double Bildungsroman." *Novel: A Forum on Fiction* 17 (1983): 28–43.

Contrasts the female with the male bildungsroman and proposes a third, distinctive tradition, the double bildungsroman, which depicts a boy and a girl growing up as a pair. Considers Emily Brontë's *Wuthering Heights*, George Eliot's *Mill on the Floss*, Willa Cather's *My Ántonia*, Jean Stafford's *Mountain Lion*, and Joyce Carol Oates's *Them*.

25. Gubar, Susan. "The Birth of the Artist as Heroine: (Re)production, the *Künstlerroman* Tradition, and the Fiction of Katherine Mansfield." *The Representation of Women in Fiction*. Ed. Carolyn G. Heilbrun and Margaret R. Higonnet. Baltimore: Johns Hopkins UP, 1983. 19–59.

Relates physical childbirth to female literary creation, notes the "startling centrality of childbearing in the *Künstlerromane* of women," and explores these elements in the fiction of Katherine Mansfield, Virginia Woolf, Alice Walker, Sylvia Plath, and others.

26.   Hansen, Elaine Tuttle. "Marge Piercy: The Double Narrative Structure of *Small Changes*." *Contemporary American Women Writers: Narrative Strategies*. Ed. Catherine Rainwater and William J. Scheick. Lexington: UP of Kentucky, 1985. 209–28.

Suggests that Piercy's novel juxtaposes a feminist inversion of the classic male structure of the bildungsroman (Beth's story) to a soap-opera structure conveying "ordinary women's experience" (Miriam's story).

27.   Howe, Susanne. "Geraldine Endsor Jewsbury." *Wilhelm Meister and His English Kinsmen: Apprentices to Life*. New York: Columbia UP, 1930; AMS, 1966. 238–52.

Explores *Zoe: Or, The History of Two Lives* as a double bildungsroman. Describes *The Half Sisters* as blazing a new path by depicting the only woman apprentice in fiction until Moore's Esther Waters and Hardy's Tess.

✳28.   Lee, Dorothy H. "The Quest for Self: Triumph and Failure in the Works of Toni Morrison." *Black Women Writers (1950–1980): A Critical Evaluation*. Ed. Mari Evans. Garden City: Anchor-Doubleday, 1984. 346–70.

Does not mention "bildungsroman" but explores the theme of quest for the self in the context of the individual's relationship with the community in *The Bluest Eye*, *Sula*, *Song of Solomon*, and *Tar Baby*.

29.   Mahlendorf, Ursula R. "Kate Chopin's *The Awakening*: Engulfment and Diffusion." *The Wellsprings of Creation: An Analysis of Male and Female "Artist Stories" from the German Romantics to American Writers of the Present*. Studies in German Literature, Linguistics, and Culture 18. Columbia: Camden House, 1985. 147–59.

Theorizes that the female artist story is not simply a counterpart of the male oedipal conflict since the mother figure assumes a constraining, negating role instead of representing the authority and mastery that must be overcome and replaced. Uses Chopin's novel to show how the female artist's quest for "the fusion experience" can end in failure.

30.   ———. "Sylvia Plath's *The Bell Jar*: The Malignant Symbiosis." *The Wellsprings of Creation: An Analysis of Male and Female "Artist Stories" from the German Romantics to American Writers of the Present*. Studies in German Literature, Linguistics, and Culture 18. Columbia: Camden House, 1985. 160–86.

Depicts Plath's work as an unsuccessful attempt to draw therapeutic inspiration from her own artistic creation and suggests the existence of a symbiotic relation between the artist and "the work of art as a transitional object."

✗ 31.   Morgan, Ellen. "Humanbecoming: Form and Focus in the Neo-Feminist Novel." *Images of Women in Fiction: Feminist Perspectives*. Ed. Susan Koppelman Cornillon. Bowling Green: Bowling Green U Popular P, 1972. 183–205. Rpt. in *Feminist Criticism: Essays on Theory, Poetry and Prose*. Ed. Cheryl L. Brown and Karen Olson. Metuchen: Scarecrow, 1978. 272–78.

Sees the bildungsroman as the most salient of three forms being used by neofeminist novelists (the others being the historical and the propaganda novels), because it allows the portrayal of woman as neofeminists see her: "in the process of becoming." Analyzes Virginia Woolf's *Orlando*, June Arnold's *Applesauce*, and Alix Kates Shulman's *Memoirs of an Ex-Prom Queen* as androgynous depictions intended to subvert sex-role stereotyping.

✗ 32.   Pratt, Annis, and Barbara White. "The Novel of Development." *Archetypal Patterns in Women's Fiction*. Bloomington: Indiana UP, 1981. 13–37.

Identifies three archetypal narrative patterns found in female bildungsromane: the green world, the rape trauma, and growing up grotesque. Sees the protagonist as external to society from the outset and regards her development as "growing down" rather than "growing up." Refers to nearly thirty novels and stories ranging from Ann Radcliffe's *Mysteries of Udolpho* to Tillie Olsen's *Yonnondio*.

33.   Sandbach-Dahlstrom, Catherine. "Woman as Christian Hero: *Heartsease* and *Hopes and Fears* as Mutations of the 'Bildungsroman.'" *Be Good Sweet Maid: Charlotte Yonge's Domestic Fiction—A Study in Dogmatic Purpose and Fictional Form*. Stockholm Studies in English 59. Stockholm: Almqvist, 1984. 111–35.

Applies Annis Pratt's concept of the conservative female bildungsroman to an analysis of *Heartsease* and *Hopes and Fears*. Believes the novels use opposite approaches to convey woman's recognition of societal restrictions and of the "denial of full adulthood."

34.   Secor, Cynthia. "*Ida*, a Great American Novel." *Fiction by American Women: Recent Views*. Ed. Winifred Farrant Bevilacqua. Port Washington: National University Publications, Associated Faculty P, 1983. 67–76.

Identifies Gertrude Stein's novel as a bildungsroman that portrays "the self-actualization of the female person" but that does not reflect conventional maturation and crises of identity.

35.   Spacks, Patricia Meyer. "The Adolescent as Heroine." *The Female Imagination*. New York: Knopf, 1975. 113–58.

Discusses several novels about young girls growing up and experiencing "serious moral change," but finds no female equivalent to James Joyce's *Portrait of the Artist as a Young Man* or J. D. Salinger's *Catcher in the Rye* because of the societal restraints on women. Considers Jane Austen's *Pride and Preju-*

dice and *Emma*, Fanny Burney's *Camilla*, Emily Brontë's *Wuthering Heights*, Sylvia Plath's *Bell Jar*, and Doris Lessing's *Martha Quest*.

36.   Stouck, David. "Willa Cather's Portrait of the Artist." *Willa Cather's Imagination*. Lincoln: U of Nebraska P, 1975. 171–205.

Discusses the conflict between art and life in several of Cather's works and considers *The Song of the Lark* a traditional *Künstlerroman* comparable to James Joyce's *Portrait of the Artist as a Young Man*.

Articles in Periodicals

37. Bader, Rudolf. "Christina Stead and the Bildungsroman." *World Literature Written in English* 23 (1984): 31–39.
Discusses *The Man Who Loved Children, For Love Alone,* and *Letty Fox: Her Luck* as a trilogy forming a single bildungsroman.

38. Baines, Barbara J. "*Villette,* a Feminist Novel." *Victorians Institute Journal* 5 (1976): 51–59.
Omitting the term *bildungsroman,* Baines analyzes Charlotte Brontë's *Villette* as "an account of the narrator's gradual discovery and attainment of personal power and self-reliance through an educative process particularly meaningful to women."

39. Bakerman, Jane S. "Cordelia Gray: Apprentice and Archetype." *Clues: A Journal of Detection* 5.1 (1984): 101–14.
Suggests that P. D. James's *Unsuitable Job for a Woman* constitutes one of a new type of bildungsroman whose protagonist follows the Persephone prototype by achieving her goals without making compromises.

40. ———. "Failures of Love: Female Initiation in the Novels of Toni Morrison." *American Literature* 52 (1981): 541–53.
Regards Morrison's novels *The Bluest Eye, Sula,* and *Song of Solomon* as combining the initiation theme and the search for love. Concludes that the ultimate alienation of the female characters reflects the failure of the initiation experience that is typical of black women in a white, male-dominated society.

41. ———. "*Lessons*: Lee Zacharia's Hoosier *Bildungsroman* as Confessional Novel." *Great Lakes Review: A Journal of Midwest Culture* 9.2 (1983): 31–36.
Discusses Zacharia's novel as the expert combination of two forms, the female bildungsroman and the confessional novel.

42.   Barnouw, Dagmar. "Disorderly Company: From *The Golden Notebook*
to *The Four-Gated City.*" *Contemporary Literature* 14 (1973): 491–514.
Rpt. in *Doris Lessing: Critical Studies.* Ed. Annis Pratt and L. S. Dembo.
Madison: U of Wisconsin P, 1974. 74–97. Rpt. in *Contemporary Women
Novelists: A Collection of Critical Essays.* Ed. Patricia Meyer Spacks.
Twentieth Century Views. Englewood Cliffs: Prentice, 1977. 30–54.
Traces the change in narrative form in Doris Lessing's two works and the
corresponding changes in the protagonist. Regards *The Four-Gated City* but
not *The Golden Notebook* as a bildungsroman.

43.   Baruch, Elaine Hoffman. "The Feminine Bildungsroman: Education
through Marriage." *Massachusetts Review* 22 (1981): 335–57.
Considers novels by both men and women and concludes that the portrayal
of the restrictive but inevitable experience of marriage makes them bildungsromane manqué and that "the authentic feminine *bildungsroman* remains to be
written." Includes Jane Austen's *Emma*, Charlotte Brontë's *Jane Eyre*, and
George Eliot's *Middlemarch*.

44.   Bell, Millicent. "Portrait of the Artist as a Young Woman." *Virginia
Quarterly Review* 61 (1976): 670–86.
Analyzes Virginia Woolf's writings for reflections of the author's "journey
towards selfhood." Commences with *The Voyage Out* as a portrait of the author as emerging artist and proceeds with *Night and Day, Jacob's Room, To
the Lighthouse*, and the first published volumes of her letters.

45.   Benson, James D. "*Romola* and the Individuation Process." *Colby Library Quarterly* 14.2 (1978): 54–71.
Does not use the term *bildungsroman* but aims to show through a Jungian
analysis of George Eliot's novel that "Romola's personality by clearly defined
stages develops significantly in breadth and depth."

46.   Boss, Judith. "The Season of Becoming: Ann Maxwell's *Change*."
Science-Fiction Studies 12.1 (35) (1985): 51–65.
Analyzes Maxwell's science fiction novel as an example of the female bildungsroman as defined by Ellen Morgan and regards it as "a specifically Jungian
account of a dissociated personality in the process of individuation."

47.   Braendlin, Bonnie Hoover. "Alther, Atwood, Ballantyne, and Gray: Secu-
lar Salvation in the Contemporary Feminist Bildungsroman." *Frontiers:
A Journal of Women Studies* 4.1 (1979): 18–22.
Suggests that Lisa Alther's *Kinflicks*, Margaret Atwood's *Lady Oracle*, Sheila
Ballantyne's *Norma Jean the Termite Queen*, and Francine du Plessix Gray's
Lovers and Tyrants "illustrate present directions of the secular feminist bildungs-
roman, an expression of modern woman's frustrating, painful, but ultimately
successful journey to freedom."

48.   ———. "Bildung in Ethnic Women Writers." *Denver Quarterly* 17 (1983): 75–87.

Discusses female bildungsromane in the light of racism as well as sexism, focusing on Louise Meriwether's *Daddy Was a Number Runner*, Alice Walker's *Meridian*, and Isabella Rios's *Victuum*.

49.   ———. "New Directions in the Contemporary *Bildungsroman*: Lisa Alther's *Kinflicks*." *Women and Literature* ns 1 (1980): 160–71.

Using Alther's novel as an example, Braendlin describes the revival and transformation of the traditional bildungsroman to meet the need of twentieth-century women authors for "a new definition of woman."

50.   Brett, Judith. "The Process of Becoming: Antigone Kefala's *The First Journey* and *The Island*." *Meanjin* 44.1 (1985): 125–33.

Compares Greek-Australian Kefala's two bildungsromane and finds *The Island* with its female protagonist more original than *The First Journey* with its traditional male protagonist and European setting.

51.   Bromberg, Pamela S. "Narrative in Drabble's *The Middle Ground*: Relativity versus Teleology." *Contemporary Literature* 24 (1983): 463–79.

Suggests that by moving toward the synchronic structure of multiple perspectives in *The Middle Ground* Margaret Drabble is leaving behind the single-identity bildungsroman structure of her earlier novels.

52.   Brown, Caroline O. "Dwindling into a Wife: A Jane Austen Heroine Grows Up." *International Journal of Women's Studies* 5 (1982): 460–69.

Observes that while all Austen's heroines develop from girlhood to womanhood, those in *Pride and Prejudice* and *Emma* diminish from happy, spirited girls to subdued, submissive women.

53.   Butcher, M. K. "From 'Maurice Guest' to 'Martha Quest': The Female Bildungsroman in Commonwealth Literature." *World Literature Written in English* 21 (1980): 254–62.

Asserts that "the history of the Commonwealth novel . . . is very much a history of female bildungsromane" but that the wide thematic variation makes the form distinct from the traditional European model. Discusses numerous Commonwealth authors, from Henry Handel Richardson to Doris Lessing.

54.   Campbell, Josie P. "The Woman as Hero in Margaret Atwood's *Surfacing*." *Mosaic* 11.3 (1978): 17–28.

Analyzes the novel's use of "the mythic heroic quest" to enlarge the protagonist's self-awareness.

55.   Carr, Glynis. "Storytelling as *Bildung* in Zora Neale Hurston's *Their Eyes Were Watching God*." *College Language Association Journal* 31 (1987): 189–200.

Assesses Hurston's bildungsroman from an interdisciplinary perspective that elucidates "the heroine's increasing verbal competence and final mastery of storytelling, both as artistic performance and as affirmation of personal and cultural identity."

X 56.   Christ, Carol P. "Margaret Atwood: The Surfacing of Women's Spiritual Quest and Vision." *Signs* 2 (1976): 316–30.

Distinguishes between the spiritual and the social quests, identifies Margaret Atwood's novel *Surfacing* as an illustration of the former, and urges feminist critics not to ignore the importance of the spiritual perception of reality in the "challenge . . . to traditional social and political structures."

57.   Collard, John L. "Identity, Conformity and the Getting of Wisdom." *Westerly* 2 (1977): 67–71.

Traces the protagonist's path to acceptance of her own individuality in Henry Handel Richardson's *Getting of Wisdom*.

58.   Davidson, Cathy N. "To Bee or Not to Bee." *Canadian Literature* 105 (1985): 197–200.

Describes Ann Rosenberg's *Bee Book* as "awesome," "intimidating," and "postmodernist" and classifies it as "a *bildungsroman*, quintessentially a novel of education."

59.   DeJong, Mary Gosselink. "*Romola*: A *Bildungsroman* for Feminists?" *South Atlantic Review* 49.4 (1984): 75–90.

Asks whether George Eliot's novel is a feminist work and concludes, "If a feminist is one who believes that everyone should be encouraged to reach his or her full potential, *Romola* is indeed a feminist work."

60.   Duncan, Erika. "Coming of Age in the Thirties: A Portrait of Tillie Olsen." *Book Forum* 6 (1982): 207–22.

Describes Olsen's life in relation to her novel *Yonnondio*, "a kind of portrait of the artist as a young woman."

61.   Federico, Annette R. "The Waif at the Window: Emily Brontë's Feminine Bildungsroman." *Victorian Newsletter* 68 (1985): 26–28.

Regards the maturation of Catherine's daughter, Cathy, in *Wuthering Heights* as a bildungsroman story that is truer than Heathcliff's.

⋇ 62.   Felski, Rita. "The Novel of Self-Discovery: A Necessary Fiction?" *Southern Review* 19 (1986): 131–48.

Correlates the popularity of the feminist bildungsroman in recent American women's literature with the rise of feminism and its assertion of female self and identity. Considers this new form a revised version of the traditional male bildungsroman since the heroine cannot achieve true fulfillment and integration in a male-dominated society but can recognize and assert her presence.

In Canada and Western Europe, where feminism has been less visible, Felski considers that a related genre, the novel of awakening, is more prominent. Believes that the novel of self-discovery reflects "the historical process of women coming to consciousness of female identity as a potentially oppositional force to existing social and cultural values." Refers to numerous novels of the 1970s and 1980s, including Margaret Atwood's *Surfacing*, Joan Barfoot's *Gaining Ground*, Marilyn French's *Women's Room*, Maxine Hong Kingston's *Woman Warrior*, Marge Piercy's *Small Changes* and *Fly Away Home*, and Alice Walker's *Color Purple*.

63.   Ferguson, Mary Anne. "The Female Novel of Development and the Myth of Psyche." *Denver Quarterly* 17.4 (1983): 58–74. Also in *The Voyage In: Fictions of Female Development*. Ed. Elizabeth Abel, Marianne Hirsch, and Elizabeth Langland. Hanover: UP of New England for Dartmouth Coll., 1983. 228–43.

Notices a pattern appearing recently in works by women and compares it with that of the classic male bildungsroman and the myth of Psyche, using as examples Eudora Welty's "At the Landing," Lisa Alther's *Kinflicks*, and Erica Jong's *Fanny, Being the True History of the Adventures of Fanny Hackabout-Jones*.

64.   Franklin, C. "The Female *Künstlerroman*, Richardson versus Bjornson." *Southerly: A Review of Australian Literature* 43 (1983): 422–36.

Analyzes Henry Handel Richardson's *Getting of Wisdom* as a subversive and disillusioned response to its literary model, *Fiskerjenten*, by Bjornstjerne Bjornson.

65.   Fulton, E. Margaret. "*Jane Eyre*: The Development of a Female Consciousness." *English Studies in Canada* 5 (1979): 432–47.

Likens Charlotte Brontë's novel to nineteenth-century spiritual autobiographies rather than to the gothic romance or other novel forms. Describes Jane Eyre's search for self as "the pilgrimage of a woman from the insecurity and dependence of childhood to the maturity and independence of adulthood." Attributes the successful journey to Jane's firm resistance to the appeal and authority of the male characters.

66.   Gaillard, Dawson. "*Gone with the Wind* as *Bildungsroman*: Or, Why Did Rhett Butler Really Leave Scarlett O'Hara?" *Georgia Review* 28 (1974): 9–18.

Suggests that Margaret Mitchell's novel is a bildungsroman in which Scarlett's "maturation from a petulant girl to a reflective adult" reflects the divergence between the myth of the Southern Lady and the concept of the New Woman.

67.   Gelfant, Blanche H. "Revolutionary Turnings: *The Mountain Lion* Reread." *Massachusetts Review* 20 (1979): 117–25. Rpt. in *The Voyage In: Fictions of Female Development*. Ed. Elizabeth Abel, Marianne Hirsch, and Elizabeth Langland. Hanover: UP of New England for

Dartmouth Coll., 1983. 149–60. Rpt. in *Women Writing in America*. By Blanche H. Gelfant. Hanover: UP of New England for Dartmouth Coll., 1984. 45–58.

Describes Jean Stafford's work as a subversion of several familiar novelistic forms, including the bildungsroman, since her characters are caught in revolutions of time, plot, and impulse.

68.   Ginsberg, Elaine. "The Female Initiation Theme in American Literature." *Studies in American Fiction* 3.1 (1975): 27–37.

Stating that the theme did not exist before the twentieth century, Ginsberg concludes that even now initiation generally means disillusionment and regret for women. Discusses Carson McCullers's *Member of the Wedding* and *The Heart Is a Lonely Hunter* and stories by Eudora Welty and Katherine Anne Porter.

69.   Gohlman, Susan A. "Martha Hesse of *The Four-Gated City*: A *Bildungsroman* Already behind Her." *South Atlantic Bulletin* 43.4 (1978): 95–106.

Describes Doris Lessing's novel, the fifth in *The Children of Violence* series, as breaking with the traditional *Bildungsprozess* since the heroine rejects "the identity which she has created out of these experiences" and begins a second apprenticeship at middle age.

70.   Gonzalez-Berry, Erlinda, and Tey Diana Rebolledo. "Growing Up Chicano: Tomás Rivera and Sandra Cisneros." *Revista Chicana-Riquena* 13.3–4 (1985): 109–19.

Contrasts the male with the female bildungsroman by comparing Rivera's *. . . y no se lo tragó* with Cisneros's *House on Mango St.*

71.   Goodman, Charlotte. "Portrait of the *Artiste Manqué* by Three Women Novelists." *Frontiers* 5 (1980): 57–59.

Does not use the term *Künstlerroman* but considers three novels about frustrated artists as reflections of the writers' awareness of "the insurmountable difficulties faced by women artists in a patriarchal society." Discusses Rebecca Harding Davis's *Life in the Iron Mills*, Edith Summers Kelley's *Weeds*, and Harriette Arnow's *Dollmaker*.

✗ 72.   Gullette, Margaret Morganroth. "Ugly Ducklings and Swans: Margaret Drabble's Fable of Progress in the Middle Years." *Modern Language Quarterly* 44 (1983): 285–304.

Noting Drabble's fascination with the myth of transformation, Gullette states that "the *Bildungsroman* was and is her literary form." Considers the female protagonists in *The Waterfall*, *Jerusalem the Golden*, *The Needle's Eye*, and *Realms of Gold* and the male protagonist in *The Ice Age*.

73.   Horne, Margot. "Portrait of the Artist as a Young Woman: The Dualism of Heroine and Anti-heroine in *Villette*." *Dutch Quarterly Review of Anglo-American Letters* 6 (1976): 216–32.

Sees the plot in Charlotte Brontë's novel as a double narrative paralleling the development of Paulina as heroine and Lucy Snowe as antiheroine. Contrasts Paulina's story of triumphant self-fulfillment with Lucy's story of repression and tortured self-discovery.

74. Kaplan, Sydney Janet. "The Limits of Consciousness in the Novels of Doris Lessing." *Contemporary Literature* 14 (1973): 536–49. Rpt. in *Doris Lessing: Critical Studies*. Ed. Annis Pratt and L. S. Dembo. Madison: U of Wisconsin P, 1974. 119–32.

Traces "the evolution towards a universal consciousness" in *Children of Violence* and contrasts that quest with the protagonist's search for individuality in the more typical bildungsroman.

75. Keyser, Elizabeth Lennox. "Alcott's Portraits of the Artist as Little Woman." *International Journal of Women's Studies* 5 (1982): 445–59.

Suggests that Alcott's four girls in *Little Women* are "portraits of the artist" and that these characters fail after encountering the limitations of woman's sphere.

76. Kornfield, Eve, and Susan Jackson. "The Female Bildungsroman in Nineteenth-Century America: Parameters of a Vision." *Journal of American Culture* 10.4 (1987): 69–75.

Views the nineteenth-century female bildungsroman as a "subgenre of domestic fiction." Considers Louisa May Alcott's *Little Women*, Margaret Sidney's "Five Little Peppers" books, Kate Douglas Wiggin's *Rebecca of Sunnybrook Farm*, and Lucy Maud Montgomery's *Anne of Green Gables* and concludes that such fiction subverted rather than promoted traditional gender roles and relations.

77. Leseur, Geta. "One Mother, Two Daughters: The Afro-American and the Afro-Caribbean Female *Bildungsroman*." *Black Scholar* 17.2 (1986): 26–33.

Compares the function and content of several Afro-American and Afro-Caribbean novels, including *Brown Girl, Brownstones*, by Paule Marshall; *Maud Martha*, by Gwendolyn Brooks; *Crick Crack Monkey*, by Merle Hodge; and *Banana Bottom*, by Claude McKay. Finds that all the protagonists share the dual problem of being black and female but that the novelistic intent ranges from racial protest to accounts of survival.

78. Mannheimer, Monica Lauritzen. "The Search for Identity in Margaret Drabble's *The Needle's Eye*." *Dutch Quarterly Review* 5 (1976): 24–35.

Sees the search for identity as being conducted by both a male and a female character but as ending in failure for each. Suggests that "the possibility of genuine self-realization seems more remote than in any of Margaret Drabble's previous works."

✳ 79.   Mansbridge, Francis. "Search for Self in the Novels of Margaret Atwood." *Journal of Canadian Fiction* 22 (1978): 106–17.

Describes the young heroine's quest for personal fulfillment in a false society in *The Edible Woman, Surfacing,* and *Lady Oracle.*

80.   McDonnell, Jane. "'A Little Spirit of Independence': Sexual Politics and the Bildungsroman in *Mansfield Park*." *Novel: A Forum on Fiction* 17 (1984): 197–214.

Notes that the feminist critic will find "interesting issues" in Jane Austen's novel and suggests that Austen's analogy between the dependence of children and that of women in general focuses on questions of sexual politics.

81.   ———. "'Perfect Goodness' or 'The Wider Life': *The Mill on the Floss* as Bildungsroman." *Genre* 15 (1982): 379–402.

Considers Eliot's novel in the light of the "gender/genre conflict" inherent in a nineteenth-century woman writer's use of the bildungsroman structure.

82.   McDowell, Deborah E. "The Self in Bloom: Alice Walker's *Meridian*." *College Language Association Journal* 24 (1981): 262–75.

Analyzes Walker's novel as a bildungsroman that "transcends the boundaries of the female gender to embrace more universal concerns about individual autonomy, self-reliance, and self-realization."

83.   Moretti, Franco. "The Comfort of Civilization." *Representations* 12 (1985): 115–39.

Analyzes the bildungsroman as the expression of the tension between self-realization and socialization and between individuality and society, with particular reference to Goethe's *Wilhelm Meister* and Jane Austen's *Pride and Prejudice.*

✳ 84.   O'Neale, Sondra. "Race, Sex and Self: Aspects of Bildung in Select Novels by Black American Women Novelists." *MELUS: The Journal of the Society for the Study of the Multi-ethnic Literature of the United States* 9.4 (1982): 25–37.

Examines the differences between the traditional white male bildungsroman and the new form necessitated by the black female experience. Works range from Frances E. W. Harper's *Iola Leroy: Or, Shadows Uplifted* to Toni Morrison's *Bluest Eye* and *Sula.*

85.   Pannill, Linda. "Willa Cather's Artist-Heroines." *Women's Studies: An Interdisciplinary Journal* 11 (1984): 223–32.

Explains that *The Song of the Lark* and *Youth and the Bright Medusa* show Cather's resolution of the conflict between the artist's devotion to her craft and woman's conventional role, as Cather conceives of the artist in "distinctly 'womanly' terms."

X 86.   Perrakis, Phyllis Sternberg. "Portrait of the Artist as a Young Girl: Alice Munro's *Lives of Girls and Women.*" *Atlantis* 7.2 (1982): 61–67.
Considers Munro's novel a bildungsroman and a reflection of Munro's creative self.

87.   Pratt, Annis. "Women and Nature in Modern Fiction." *Contemporary Literature* 13 (1972): 476–90.
Compares male and female bildungsromane, including May Sinclair's *Mary Olivier, a Life,* Ellen Glasgow's *Barren Ground,* Willa Cather's *O Pioneers!,* Virginia Woolf's *Voyage Out,* and Doris Lessing's *Children of Violence.* Considers the "naturistic epiphany" distinctive of the female passage to maturity.

88.   Reardon, Joan. "*Fear of Flying*: Developing the Feminist Novel." *International Journal of Women's Studies* 1 (1978): 306–20. Rpt. in *Fiction by American Women: Recent Views.* Ed. Winifred Farrant Bevilacqua. Port Washington: National University Publications, Associated Faculty P, 1983. 131–43.
Describes Erica Jong's novel as conforming to the conventional bildungsroman in structure while portraying "the coming of age of the artist in the totality of female experience," above all in her coming to terms with female physiology.

89.   Rose, Ellen Cronan. "The Eriksonian Bildungsroman: An Approach through Doris Lessing." *University of Hartford Studies in Literature: A Journal of Interdisciplinary Criticism* 7 (1975): 1–17.
Suggests that the critical problems inherent in Lessing's *Four-Gated City* as a "post-classical *Bildungsroman*" can be resolved by applying Eriksonian psychology to its protagonist.

90.   Rosowski, Susan J. "The Novel of Awakening." *Genre* 12 (1979): 313–32. Rpt. in *The Voyage In: Fictions of Female Development.* Ed. Elizabeth Abel, Marianne Hirsch, and Elizabeth Langland. Hanover: UP of New England for Dartmouth Coll., 1983. 49–68.
Sees the theme of awakening as a particular development of the bildungsroman in literature by and about women. Discusses Gustave Flaubert's *Madame Bovary,* Kate Chopin's *Awakening,* Willa Cather's *My Mortal Enemy,* Agnes Smedley's *Daughter of Earth,* and George Eliot's *Middlemarch.*

91.   Ross, Catherine Sheldrick. " 'A Singing Spirit': Female Rites of Passage in *Klee Wyck, Surfacing* and *The Diviners.*" *Atlantis* 4.1 (1978): 86–94.
Discusses works by the Canadian novelists Emily Carr, Margaret Atwood, and Margaret Laurence and each heroine's experience of "tribal rituals of initiation" to achieve wholeness or self-discovery.

92.   Schvey, Henry I. "Sylvia Plath's *The Bell Jar*: Bildungsroman or Case History." *Dutch Quarterly Review of Anglo-American Letters* 8 (1977): 18–37.

Objects to the tendency of critics since 1963 to obscure Plath's work by a preoccupation with her life and death. Analyzes the artistic elements of her novel and the incorporation of autobiographical factors but excludes references to her suicide.

93.   Stein, Karen F. "*Meridian*: Alice Walker's Critique of Revolution." *Black American Literature Forum* 20.1–2 (1986): 129–41.

Sees Walker's novel as a bildungsroman in which the protagonist "is the embodiment of a new consciousness" that reflects the transformation of the author's philosophical stance from 1960s revolutionary activism to affirmation of the female self in a patriarchal society.

94.   Stewart, Grace. "Mother, Daughter, and the Birth of the Female Artist." *Women's Studies* 6 (1979): 127–45.

Considers the female *Künstlerroman* from the perspective of the mother-daughter-artist relationship and the Demeter and Persephone myth. Novels range from Elizabeth Stuart Phelps Ward's *Story of Avis* to Virginia Woolf's *To the Lighthouse* and Esther M. Broner's *Her Mothers*.

95.   Struthers, J. B. "Reality and Ordering: The Growth of a Young Artist in *Lives of Girls and Women*." *Essays on Canadian Writing* 3 (1975): 32–46.

Closely compares Alice Munro's novel to James Joyce's *Portrait of the Artist as a Young Man* and demonstrates that Joyce's novel was the model for Munro's *Künstlerroman*.

96.   Tiger, Virginia. "The Female Novel of Education and the Confessional Heroine." *Dalhousie Review* 60 (1980): 472–86.

Evaluates Doris Lessing's *Golden Notebook* as part of a tradition of morally didactic novels written by women for women since the eighteenth century. Calls Fanny Burney's *Evelina: Or, A Young Lady's Entrance into the World* the "first feminine *bildungsroman*."

97.   Vincent, Sybil Korff. "In the Crucible: The Forging of an Identity as Demonstrated in Didion's *Play It As It Lays*." *Perspectives on Contemporary Literature* 3 (1977): 58–64.

Focuses on the relationship between the individual and the community while tracing the journey of the heroine through several hostile communities. Observes that integration into the community is impossible until the heroine defines her worth, her values, and her own direction.

98.   Voloshin, Beverly R. "The Limits of Domesticity: The Female Bildungsroman in America, 1820–1870." *Women's Studies: An Interdisciplinary Journal* 10 (1984): 283–302.

Proposes that the female bildungsroman reflected the tension between the nineteenth-century "cult of domesticity" and the spreading theory of the natural rights of individual liberty and equality. Refers to Catharine Sedgwick's *New-England Tale*, Susan Warner's *Wide, Wide World*, Maria Cummins's *Lamplighter*, and Augusta Jane Evans's *Beulah*, among others.

99.   Wagner, Linda W. "Plath's *The Bell Jar* as Female *Bildungsroman*." *Women's Studies: An Interdisciplinary Journal* 12 (1986): 55-68.

Using Jerome Buckley's definition, Wagner analyzes Sylvia Plath's *Bell Jar* as a "highly conventional *bildungsroman*" but concludes by contrasting the female with the male experience of *Bildung*.

100.   Waxman, Barbara Frey. "From *Bildungsroman* to *Reifungsroman*: Aging in Doris Lessing's Fiction." *Soundings: An Interdisciplinary Journal* 68 (1985): 318-34.

Coins a new term, *Reifungsroman*, to identify a particularly female variant of the bildungsroman in which the protagonist experiences "ripening and maturing in an emotional and philosophical way." Applies the term to Lessing's novels *The Summer before the Dark* and *The Diary of a Good Neighbor*.

101.   ———. "Heart, Mind, Body, and Soul: George Eliot's Female Bildungsroman." *Victorians Institute Journal* 11 (1983): 61-82.

After a lengthy analysis of *The Mill on the Floss* and *Middlemarch*, concludes that for Eliot's women self-discovery and "the art of living" mean recognizing the limitations of reality and the need for inner resources.

102.   Weir, Sybil. "*The Morgesons*: A Neglected Feminist Bildungsroman." *New England Quarterly: A Historical Review of New England Life and Letters* 49 (1976): 427-39.

States that this "virtually unknown nineteenth-century novel" by Elizabeth Drew Barstow Stoddard "features a heroine who passionately undertakes the voyage of self-discovery and firmly rejects the established social institutions."

103.   Wells, Susan. "Self-Cultivation, Political Reaction, and the *Bildungsroman*." *Minnesota Review* 13 (1979): 71-97.

Explores "how self-culture has been pursued in previous periods of reaction and the ways in which this process can be represented in literature," specifically in Stendhal's *Chartreuse de Parme*, Doris Lessing's *Four-Gated City*, and Jerry Rubin's *Growing (Up) at Thirty-Seven*.

104.   Zagarell, Sandra A. "The Repossession of a Heritage: Elizabeth Stoddard's *The Morgesons*." *Studies in American Fiction* 13.1 (1985): 45-56.

Regards Stoddard's novel as a critique of both gender and genre limitations: of societal restrictions on female self-development on the one hand and of "the masculine shape of the *Bildungsroman*" on the other.

105.   Zajdel, Melody M. "Portrait of an Artist as a Woman: H. D.'s Raymonde Ransom." *Women's Studies: An Interdisciplinary Journal* 13.1-2 (1986): 127-34.

Explores H. D.'s fictional character, Raymonde Ransom, who appears in the novel *Palimpsest* and the story "Narthex." Believes Ransom partly autobiographical and also "an articulate statement by a major feminist modernist writer about the problems and powers inherent in becoming a modern woman writer."

106.   Zilboorg, Caroline. "Women before World War I: An Exploration of Their Awakening in the College Novel." *Great Lakes Review: A Journal of Midwest Culture* 7.2 (1981): 29–38.

Considers several college novels with reference to the bildungsroman tradition, including Dorothea Frances Caufield Fisher's *Bent Twig* and Honoré McCue Willsie Morrow's *Lydia of the Pines*.

Abstracts in *Dissertation Abstracts International (DAI)*

107. Baer, Elizabeth Roberts. "'The Pilgrimage Inward': The Quest Motif in the Fiction of Margaret Atwood, Doris Lessing, and Jean Rhys." *DAI* 42 (1982): 3606A. Indiana U.

108. Bick, Suzann. "Towards a Female *Bildungsroman*: The Protagonist in the Works of Elizabeth Gaskell." *DAI* 39 (1979): 4934A. U of California, Berkeley.

109. Blakey, Barbara Fahey. "Varieties of the *Bildungsroman*: Portraits of the Self in a Changing Society." *DAI* 41 (1981): 4038A. Arizona State U.

110. Bordner, Marsha Stanfield. "The Woman as Artist in Twentieth-Century Fiction." *DAI* 40 (1980): 5438A. Ohio State U.

111. Bowers, Susan Rae Belle. "The Child as Mother of the Woman: Virginia Woolf's Female *Bildungsromane*." *DAI* 42 (1982): 3607A. U of Oregon.

112. Gaston, Karen Carmean. "The Theme of Female Self-Discovery in the Novels of Judith Rossner, Gail Godwin, Alice Walker, and Toni Morrison." *DAI* 41 (1980): 1053A. Auburn U.

113. Goldberg, Raquel Prado-Totaro. "The Artist Fiction of James, Wharton, and Cather." *DAI* 36 (1976): 4475A. Northwestern U.

114. Hammer, Andrea Gale. "Recitations of the Past: Identity in Novels by Edith Wharton, Ellen Glasgow, and Carson McCullers." *DAI* 42 (1982): 5121–22A. U of California, Davis.

115. Hovet, Grace O'Neill. "The *Bildungsroman* of the Middle-Aged Woman: Her Emergence as Heroine in British Fiction since 1920." *DAI* 37 (1977): 5142A. U of Kansas.

116. Huf, Linda. "Portrait of the Artist as a Young Woman: The Female *Künstlerromane* in America." *DAI* 42 (1982): 3600A. U of Maryland.

117. Jacobs, Maureen Sheehan. "Beyond the Castle: The Development of the Paradigmatic Female Story." *DAI* 41 (1980): 679A. American U.

118. Krause, Janet Boettcher. "Self-Actualizing Women in Willa Cather's Prairie Novels." *DAI* 39 (1979): 6132a. U of Nebraska, Lincoln.

119. Labovitz, Esther K. "The Female *Bildungsroman* in the Twentieth Century: A Comparative Study: Dorothy Richardson, Simone de Beauvoir, Doris Lessing, Christa Wolf." *DAI* 43 (1983): 2341–42A. New York U.

120. LeSeur, Geta J. "The *Bildungsroman* in Afro-American and Afro-Caribbean Fiction: An Integrated Consciousness." *DAI* 43 (1983): 2681A. Indiana U.

121. Lukens, Cynthia Diane. "The Woman Artist's Journey: Self-Consciousness in the Novels of Virginia Woolf." *DAI* 42 (1981): 1648–49a. U of Washington.

122. McGowan, Marcia Phillips. "Patterns of Female Experience in Eudora Welty's Fiction." *DAI* 38 (1977): 788A. Rutgers U.

123. Mecke, Mary Amanda. " 'So Hard to Write': Women Artists in Women's Novels from Woolf to Lessing and Drabble." *DAI* 45 (1984): 1409A. U of California, Los Angeles.

124. Osborne, Marianne Muse. "The Hero and Heroine in the British *Bildungsroman*: *David Copperfield* and *A Portrait of the Artist as a Young Man, Jane Eyre* and *The Rainbow*." *DAI* 32 (1972): 4013–14A. Tulane U.

125. Pannill, Linda. "The Artist-Heroine in American Fiction, 1890–1920." *DAI* 37 (1976): 1551A. U of North Carolina, Chapel Hill.

126. Parker, Pamela Lorraine. "The Search for Autonomy in the Works of Kate Chopin, Ellen Glasgow, Carson McCullers, and Shirley Ann Grau." *DAI* 43 (1982): 454A. Rice U.

127. Perry, Constance Marie. "Adolescence, Autonomy, and Vocation: Heroines of *Künstlerromane* by Modern American Women." *DAI* 43 (1983): 2669–70A. Indiana U.

128.   Plender, Martha Holman. "Virginia Woolf and the Woman Artist: A Study of a Tradition in Transformation." *DAI* 45 (1985): 2115A. U of California, San Diego.

129.   Richardi, Janis Marie. "The Modern British *Bildungsroman* and the Woman Novelist: Dorothy Richardson, May Sinclair, Rosamond Lehmann, Elizabeth Bowen, and Doris Lessing." *DAI* 42 (1982): 3612–13A. U of North Carolina, Chapel Hill.

130.   Rose, Ellen C. "Doris Lessing's *Children of Violence* as a Bildungsroman: An Eriksonian Analysis." *DAI* 35 (1974): 3006–07A. U of Massachusetts.

131.   Shabka, Margaret Collins. "The Writer's Search for Identity: A Redefinition of the Feminine Personality from Virginia Woolf to Margaret Drabble and Doris Lessing." *DAI* 42 (1982): 3613A. Kent State U.

132.   Sommers, Jeffrey David. "Setting and the Search for Identity: The Victorian Maturation Novel." *DAI* 41 (1981): 5112A. New York U.

133.   Turner, Gordon Philip. "The Protagonists' Initiatory Experiences in the Canadian *Bildungsroman*: 1908–1971." *DAI* 40 (1979): 2057–58A. U of British Columbia.

Female Bildungsromane

Novels of self-discovery written in English by women and cited in the critical works listed above.

Adams, Alice. *Listening to Billie*. 1978.

Alcott, Louisa May. *Little Women*. 1868.

———. *Work: A Story of Experience*. 1873.

Alther, Lisa. *Kinflicks*. 1975.

Arnold, June. *Applesauce*. 1966.

———. *The Cook and the Carpenter*. 1973.

———. *Sister Gin*. 1975.

Arnow, Harriet. *The Dollmaker*. 1953.

———. *The Weedkiller's Daughter*. 1970.

Atwood, Margaret. *The Edible Woman*. 1969.

———. *Lady Oracle*. 1976.

———. *Surfacing*. 1972.

Austen, Jane. *Emma*. 1816.

———. *Mansfield Park*. 1814.

———. *Northanger Abbey*. 1818.

———. *Persuasion*. 1818.

———. *Pride and Prejudice*. 1813.

Austin, Mary Hunter. *Outland*. 1919.

———. *A Woman of Genius*. 1912.

Ballantyne, Sheila. *Norma Jean the Termite Queen*. 1975.

Barfoot, Joan. *Gaining Ground*. 1978.

Bawden, Nina. *A Woman of My Age*. 1967.

Bowen, Elizabeth. *The Death of the Heart*. 1938.

Broner, Esther M. *Her Mothers*. 1975.

Brontë, Charlotte. *Jane Eyre*. 1847.

———. *The Professor*. 1857.

———. *Shirley*. 1849.

———. *Villette*. 1853.

Brontë, Emily. *Wuthering Heights*. 1847.

Brooks, Gwendolyn. *Maud Martha*. 1953.

Brown, Rita Mae. *Rubyfruit Jungle*. 1973.

Bryant, Dorothy. *Ella Price's Journal*. 1972.

Burney, Fanny. *Camilla: Or, A Picture of Youth*. 1796.

———. *Evelina: Or, A Young Lady's Entrance into the World*. 1778.

———. *The Wanderer*. 1814.

Bussy, Dorothy (Strachey). *Olivia*. 1949.

Byatt, A. S. *The Game*. 1967.

Caird, Mona. *The Daughters of Danaus*. 1894.

Carr, Emily. *Klee Wyck*. 1941.

Cary, Joyce. *Herself Surprised*. 1941.

Cather, Willa. *A Lost Lady*. 1924.

———. *Lucy Gayheart*. 1931.

———. *My Antonia*. 1918.

———. *My Mortal Enemy*. 1926.

———. *O Pioneers!* 1913.

———. *Obscure Destinies*. 1932.

———. *The Song of the Lark*. 1915.

———. *Youth and the Bright Medusa*. 1920.

Charles, Gerda. *A Slanting Light*. 1963.

Chesebro', Caroline. *The Children of Light: A Theme for the Time*. 1853.

——. *Isa: A Pilgrimage.* 1852.

——. *Victoria: Or, The World Overcome.* 1856.

Chopin, Kate. *The Awakening.* 1900.

Cisneros, Sandra. *The House on Mango St.* 1983.

Cummins, Maria. *The Lamplighter.* 1854.

——. *Mabel Vaughan.* 1857.

Davenport, Marcia. *Of Lena Geyer.* 1936.

Davis, Rebecca Harding. *Life in the Iron Mills.* 1861.

Didion, Joan. *Play It As It Lays.* 1970.

Dorr, Julia Caroline Ripley. *Farmingdale.* 1854.

——. *Lanmere.* 1856.

Drabble, Margaret. *Jerusalem the Golden.* 1967.

——. *The Middle Ground.* 1980.

——. *The Needle's Eye.* 1972.

——. *Realms of Gold.* 1975.

——. *A Summer's Birdcage.* 1962.

——. *The Waterfall.* 1969.

Eliot, George. *Middlemarch.* 1872.

——. *The Mill on the Floss.* 1860.

——. *Romola.* 1862–63.

Embury, Emma Catherine. *Constance Latimer: Or, The Blind Girl.* 1838.

Evans, Augusta Jane. *Beulah.* 1859.

——. *Macaria: Or, The Altars of Sacrifice.* 1864.

——. *St. Elmo: A Novel.* 1867.

Fauset, Jessie. *The Chinaberry Tree.* 1931.

——. *Comedy: American Style.* 1933.

——. *Plum Bun.* 1929.

——. *There Is Confusion.* 1924.

Fern, Fanny. *Rose Clark.* 1856.

——. *Ruth Hall.* 1855.

Fisher, Dorothea Frances Canfield. *The Bent Twig.* 1915.

Fitzgerald, Zelda. *Save Me the Waltz*. 1932.

Flanner, Janet. *The Cubicle City*. 1926.

Franklin, Miles. *My Brilliant Career*. 1901.

French, Marilyn. *The Women's Room*. 1977.

Gaskell, Elizabeth. *Cranford*. 1851–53.

——. *Mary Barton*. 1848.

——. *North and South*. 1854–55.

——. *Ruth*. 1853.

——. *Sylvia's Lovers*. 1863.

——. *Wives and Daughters*. 1864–66.

Gilman, Caroline Howard. *Love's Progress*. 1840.

——. *Recollections of a Housekeeper.* 1834.

——. *Recollections of a Southern Matron*. 1838.

Glasgow, Ellen. *Barren Ground*. 1925.

——. *The Descendant*. 1897.

——. *Phases of an Inferior Planet*. 1898.

——. *The Wheel of Life*. 1906.

Godwin, Gail. *Glass People*. 1972.

——. *The Odd Woman*. 1974.

——. *The Perfectionists*. 1970.

——. *Violet Clay*. 1978.

Gordon, Mary. *Final Payments*. 1978.

Gould, Lois. *Final Analysis*. 1974.

Grau, Shirley Ann. *The Condor Passes*. 1971.

——. *The House on Coliseum Street*. 1961.

——. *The Keepers of the House*. 1964.

Graves, A. J. *Girlhood and Womanhood*. 1844.

Gray, Francine du Plessix. *Lovers and Tyrants*. 1967.

H. D. *Palimpsest*. 1926.

Harland, Marion. *Alone*. 1854.

——. *The Hidden Path*. 1855.

Harper, Frances E. W. *Iola LeRoy: Or, Shadows Uplifted.* 1892.

Hentz, Caroline Lee. *Eoline.* 1852.

——. *Ernest Linwood.* 1856.

——. *Linda.* 1850.

——. *Rena, the Snowbird.* 1850.

Hodge, Merle. *Crick Crack Monkey.* 1970.

Holmes, Mary Jane. *Dora Deane.* 1859.

——. *The English Orphans.* 1855.

——. *Lena Rivers.* 1856.

——. *Marian Grey.* 1863.

——. *Meadow Brook.* 1857.

Hunter, Kristen. *God Bless the Child.* 1964.

——. *The Soul Brothers and Sister Lou.* 1968.

Hurston, Zora Neale. *Their Eyes Were Watching God.* 1937.

Jackson, Shirley. *Hangsaman.* 1951.

James, P. D. *Innocent Blood.* 1980.

——. *An Unsuitable Job for a Woman.* 1972.

Jewsbury, Geraldine. *The Half Sisters.* 1848.

——. *Zoe: Or, The History of Two Lives.* 1845.

Johnson, Pamela Hansford. *Catherine Carter.* 1968.

Johnston, Mary. *Hagar.* 1913.

Jones, Gayle. *Corregidora.* 1975.

Jong, Erica. *Fanny, Being the True History of the Adventures of Fanny Hackabout-Jones.* 1980.

——. *Fear of Flying.* 1973.

——. *How to Save Your Own Life.* 1977.

Kefala, Antigone. *The Island.* 1984.

Keith, Marian. *'Lisbeth of the Dale.* 1910.

Kelley, Edith Summers. *The Devil's Hand.* 1934.

——. *Weeds.* 1923.

Kingston, Maxine Hong. *The Woman Warrior.* 1977.

Larsen, Nella. *Passing*. 1929.

Laurence, Margaret. *The Diviners*. 1974.

———. *The Stone Angel*. 1964.

Lazarre, Jean. *The Mother Knot*. 1977.

Le Guin, Ursula K. *Planet of Exile*. 1966.

Lehmann, Rosamond. *Dusty Answer*. 1927.

Leslie, Eliza. *Amelia*. 1848.

Lessing, Doris. *Children of Violence*. 1952–69.

———. *The Diary of a Good Neighbor*. 1984.

———. *The Four-Gated City*. 1969.

———. *The Golden Notebook*. 1962.

———. *Martha Quest*. 1952.

———. *Memoirs of a Survivor*. 1975.

———. *The Summer before the Dark*. 1973.

Lurie, Alison. *Real People*. 1969.

Lysenko, Vera. *Yellow Boots*. 1954.

Mace, Betty W. *You Can Have It When I'm Through with It*. 1976.

Marshall, Paule. *Brown Girl, Brownstones*. 1959.

———. *Praisesong for the Widow*. 1983.

Maxwell, Ann. *Change*. 1975.

McCullers, Carson. *The Heart Is a Lonely Hunter*. 1940.

———. *A Member of the Wedding*. 1946.

McIntosh, Maria. *Charms and Counter-Charms*. 1848.

———. *The Lofty and the Lowly: Or, Good in All and None All-Good*. 1853.

———. *Two Lives: Or, To Seem and to Be*. 1846.

———. *Two Pictures: Or, What We Think of Ourselves and What the World Thinks of Us*. 1863.

———. *Violet: Or, The Cross and the Crown*. 1856.

———. *Woman an Enigma*. 1843.

Meriwether, Louise. *Daddy Was a Number Runner*. 1970.

Miller, Isabel. *Patience and Sarah*. (First published as *A Place for Us*.) 1969.

Mitchell, Margaret. *Gone with the Wind*. 1936.

Montgomery, Lucy Maud. *Anne of Green Gables*. 1908.

Morrison, Toni. *The Bluest Eye*. 1970.

——. *Song of Solomon*. 1977.

——. *Sula*. 1974.

——. *Tar Baby*. 1981.

Morrow, Honoré McCue Willsie. *Lydia of the Pines*. 1917.

Munro, Alice. *Lives of Girls and Women*. 1971.

Newman, Francis. *The Hardboiled Virgin*. 1926.

Nichols, Mary Sargeant. *Agnes Morris*. 1849.

——. *Mary Lyndon*. 1855.

Nietzke, Ann. *Windowlight*. 1981.

Oates, Joyce Carol. *Marya: A Life*. 1986.

——. *Them*. 1969.

Olsen, Tillie. *Yonnondio*. 1974.

Petesch, Natalie L. M. *The Odyssey of Katinou Kalokovich*. 1974.

Petry, Ann. *Country Place*. 1947.

——. *The Narrows*. 1953.

——. *The Street*. 1946.

Phelps, Almira Hart. *Ida Norman: Or, Trials and Their Uses*. 1848.

Piercy, Marge. *Fly Away Home*. 1985.

——. *Small Changes*. 1973.

Plath, Sylvia. *The Bell Jar*. 1963.

Porter, Katherine Anne. *Ship of Fools*. 1962.

Radcliffe, Ann. *The Mysteries of Udolpho*. 1764.

Rhys, Jean. *Wide Sargasso Sea*. 1966.

Richardson, Dorothy Miller. *Pilgrimage*. 1938.

Richardson, Henry Handel. *The End of a Childhood*. 1934.

——. *The Fortunes of Richard Mahoney*. 1917–29.

——. *The Getting of Wisdom*. 1910.

Rios, Isabella. *Victuum*. 1976.

Rosenberg, Ann. *The Bee Book*. 1982.

Rossner, Judith. *Any Minute I Can Split*. 1972.

———. *Attachments*. 1977.

———. *Looking for Mr. Goodbar*. 1975.

———. *Nine Months in the Life of an Old Maid*. 1969.

———. *To the Precipice*. 1966.

Russ, Joanna. *The Female Man*. 1975.

Sarton, May. *Kinds of Love*. 1970.

———. *Mrs. Stevens Hears the Mermaids Singing*. 1965.

Sayers, Dorothy. *Gaudy Night*. 1935.

Schreiner, Olive. *The Story of an African Farm*. 1883.

Sedgwick, Ann Douglas. *Tante*. 1911.

Sedgwick, Catharine. *Clarence*. 1830.

———. *Hope Leslie*. 1827.

———. *The Linwoods*. 1835.

———. *Married or Single?* 1857.

———. *A New-England Tale*. 1822.

———. *Redwood*. 1824.

Shulman, Alix Kates. *Memoirs of an Ex-Prom Queen*. 1972.

Sidney, Margaret. *Five Little Peppers and How They Grew*. 1881.

Sinclair, May. *The Creators*. 1910.

———. *Mary Olivier: A Life*. 1919.

Smedley, Agnes. *Daughter of Earth*. 1929.

Smith, Betty. *A Tree Grows in Brooklyn*. 1943.

Smith, Stevie. *Novel on Yellow Paper*. 1932.

———. *Over the Frontier*. 1938.

Southworth, E. D. E. N. *The Discarded Daughter*. 1852.

———. *The Hidden Hand*. 1889.

———. *Retribution*. 1849.

———. *Vivia: Or, The Secret of Power*. 1857.

Spark, Muriel. *The Comforters*. 1957.

——. *Loitering with Intent.* 1981.

——. *The Prime of Miss Jean Brodie.* 1961.

——. *The Public Image.* 1968.

Stafford, Jean. *Boston Adventure.* 1944.

——. *The Catherine Wheel.* 1952.

——. *The Mountain Lion.* 1947.

Stead, Christina. *For Love Alone.* 1944.

——. *Letty Fox: Her Luck.* 1946.

——. *The Man Who Loved Children.* 1940.

Stein, Gertrude. *Ida: A Novel.* 1941.

Stephens, Ann Sophia. *The Heiress of Greenhurst.* 1857.

——. *Mary Derwent.* 1858.

——. *The Old Homestead.* 1855.

Stephens, Harriet Marion. *Hagar: A Story of Today.* 1858.

Stoddard, Elizabeth Drew Barstow. *The Morgesons.* 1862.

Stowe, Harriet Beecher. *Ellen Parry: Or, Trials of the Heart.* 1850.

Suckow, Ruth. *The Odyssey of a Nice Girl.* 1925.

Swados, Elizabeth. *Leah and Lazar: A Novel.* 1982.

Tennenbaum, Silvia. *Rachel, the Rabbi's Wife.* 1978.

Townsend, Virginia. *While It Was Morning.* 1858.

Tuthill, Louisa C. *Reality: Or, The Millionaire's Daughter.* 1856.

Tyler, Anne. *The Accidental Tourist.* 1985.

——. *Celestial Navigation.* 1974.

——. *The Clock Winder.* 1972.

——. *Dinner at the Homesick Restaurant.* 1982.

——. *Earthly Possessions.* 1977.

——. *Morgan's Passing.* 1980.

——. *Searching for Caleb.* 1976.

Walker, Alice. *The Color Purple.* 1983.

——. *Meridian.* 1976.

Ward, Elizabeth Stuart Phelps. *The Story of Avis.* 1877.

Warner, Anna. *Dollars and Cents.* 1852.

———. *My Brother's Keeper.* 1855.

Warner, Susan. *The Hills of the Shatemuc.* 1856.

———. *Queechy.* 1852.

———. *The Wide, Wide World.* 1850.

Warner, Sylvia Townsend. *Lolly Willowes.* 1926.

Welty, Eudora. *Delta Wedding.* 1946.

———. *Losing Battles.* 1970.

———. *The Optimist's Daughter.* 1972.

Wharton, Edith. *Summer.* 1917.

Wiggin, Kate Douglas. *Rebecca of Sunnybrook Farm.* 1903.

Wilson, Ethel. *Hetty Dorval.* 1947.

Winsloe, Christa. *The Child Manuela.* 1933.

Woodbury, Helen. *The Misty Flats.* 1925.

Woolf, Virginia. *Between the Acts.* 1941.

———. *Mrs. Dalloway.* 1925.

———. *Night and Day.* 1919.

———. *Orlando.* 1928.

———. *To the Lighthouse.* 1927.

———. *The Voyage Out.* 1915.

———. *The Waves.* 1927.

Wright, Sarah. *This Child's Gonna Live.* 1969.

Yonge, Charlotte. *Heartsease: Or, The Brother's Wife.* 1854.

———. *Hopes and Fears: Or, Scenes from the Life of a Spinster.* 1860.

Young, E. H. *Miss Mole.* 1930.

Zacharia, Lee. *Lessons.* 1981.

Index

Numbers refer to citations, not pages. For a list of female bildungsromane written by particular women authors, see the section immediately preceding this index.

Abel, Elizabeth, 1
Adams, Alice, 8, 116
Adams, Marianne, 17
Alcott, Louisa May, 1, 75, 76
Alther, Lisa, 47, 49, 63
Anthony, Michael, 120
Arnold, June, 1, 31, 125
Arnow, Harriette, 5, 71, 110, 125
Atwood, Margaret, 3, 15, 22, 47, 54, 56, 62, 79, 91, 107, 117
Austen, Jane, 4, 11, 35, 43, 52, 80, 83, 117
Austin, Mary Hunter, 15, 110, 125, 127

Bachmann, Ingeborg, 1
Bader, Rudolf, 37
Baer, Elizabeth Roberts, 1, 107
Baines, Barbara J., 38
Bakerman, Jane S., 39, 40, 41
Baldwin, James, 120
Ballantyne, Sheila, 47
Barfoot, Joan, 62
Barnouw, Dagmar, 42
Baruch, Elaine Hoffman, 43
Bawden, Nina, 115
Baym, Nina, 2
Beauvoir, Simone de, 10, 119
Beebe, Maurice, 18
Bell, Millicent, 44
Bellow, Saul, 7
Benson, James D., 45
Bick, Suzann, 108
Bjornson, Bjornstjerne, 64
Blakey, Barbara Fahey, 109
Bordner, Marsha Stanfield, 110

Boss, Judith, 46
Bowen, Elizabeth, 117, 129
Bowers, Susan Rae Belle, 111
Braendlin, Bonnie Hoover, 47, 48, 49
Brett, Judith, 50
Bromberg, Pamela S., 51
Broner, Esther M., 15, 94
Brontë, Charlotte, 1, 5, 11, 12, 17, 20, 38, 43, 65, 73, 109, 117, 124, 132
Brontë, Emily, 24, 35, 61
Brooks, Gwendolyn, 1, 77, 120
Broumas, Olga, 1
Brown, Caroline O., 52
Brown, Rita Mae, 125
Browning, Elizabeth Barrett, 22, 128
Bryant, Dorothy, 8, 116
Buckler, Ernest, 133
Buckley, Jerome, 1, 19, 99
Burney, Fanny, 35, 96
Bussy, Dorothy (Strachey), 1
Butcher, M. K., 53
Butler, Samuel, 109, 132
Byatt, A. S., 123

Caird, Mona, 127
Campbell, Josie P., 54
Carlyle, Thomas, 109
Carr, Emily, 91
Carr, Glynis, 55
Carter, Angela, 1
Cary, Joyce, 115
Cather, Willa, 8, 15, 24, 36, 85, 87, 90, 110, 113, 116, 118, 125, 127, 128
Charles, Gerda, 115

Chase, Karen, 20
Chesebro', Caroline, 2
Chopin, Kate, 1, 3, 5, 8, 9, 29, 90, 116, 126
Christ, Carol P., 3, 56
Christian, Barbara, 21
Cisneros, Sandra, 70
Clarke, Austin, 120
Cohen, Leonard, 133
Collard, John L., 57
Cummins, Maria, 2, 98

Dalsimer, Katherine, 4
Davenport, Marcia, 8, 116
Davidson, Cathy N., 58
Davis, Rebecca Harding, 71
DeJong, Mary Gosselink, 59
de Staël, Mme, 18, 128
Dickens, Charles, 109, 124, 132
Didion, Joan, 97
Dorr, Julia Caroline Ripley, 2
Drabble, Margaret, 6, 7, 51, 72, 78, 117,
    123, 131
Duncan, Erika, 60
DuPlessis, Rachel Blau, 22

Edwards, Lee R., 5
Eliot, George, 1, 5, 11, 19, 24, 43, 45, 59,
    81, 90, 101, 109, 132
Ellison, Ralph, 120
Embury, Emma Catherine, 2
Erikson, Erik, 13, 89
Evans, Augusta Jane, 2, 9, 98

Fauset, Jessie, 84
Federico, Annette R., 61
Felski, Rita, 62
Ferguson, Mary Anne, 63
Fern, Fanny, 2, 8, 116
Ferrier, Carole, 23
Fisher, Dorothea Frances Canfield, 106
Fitzgerald, Zelda, 15
Flanner, Janet, 127
Flaubert, Gustave, 90
Fontane, Theodor, 1
Frank, Ann, 4
Franklin, C., 64
Franklin, Miles, 23
French, Marilyn, 62
Friedan, Betty, 110
Frieden, Sandra, 1
Frye, Joanne S., 6
Fulton, E. Margaret, 65

Gaillard, Dawson, 66
Gardner, Susan, 23

Gaskell, Elizabeth, 108
Gaston, Karen Carmean, 112
Gelfant, Blanche H., 67
Gilman, Caroline Howard, 2
Ginsberg, Elaine, 68
Glasgow, Ellen, 87, 114, 125, 126
Godwin, Gail, 6, 112
Goethe, Johann Wolfgang von, 1, 11, 13,
    83, 109
Gohlman, Susan A., 69
Goldberg, Raquel Prado-Totaro, 113
Gonzalez-Berry, Erlinda, 70
Goodman, Charlotte, 24, 71
Gordon, Mary, 117
Gould, Lois, 8, 116
Grau, Shirley Ann, 126
Graves, A. J., 2
Gray, Francine du Plessix, 47
Grove, Frederick Philip, 133
Gubar, Susan, 25
Gullette, Margaret Morganroth, 7, 72

H. D., 105
Haig-Brown, Roderick, 133
Hall, Radclyffe, 110
Hammer, Andrea Gale, 114
Hansen, Elaine Tuttle, 26
Hardy, Thomas, 27, 132
Harland, Marion, 2
Harper, Frances E. W., 21, 84
Hentz, Caroline Lee, 2
Hirsch, Marianne, 1
Hodge, Merle, 77
Holmes, Mary Jane, 2
Horne, Margot, 73
Hovet, Grace O'Neill, 115
Howe, Susanne, 18, 27
Huf, Linda, 8, 116
Hughes, Langston, 120
Hunter, Kristen, 77, 84, 120
Hurston, Zora Neale, 5, 55

Jackson, Shirley, 127
Jackson, Susan, 76
Jacobs, Maureen Sheehan, 117
James, Henry, 113
James, P. D., 39
Jewsbury, Geraldine, 18, 27
Johnson, Pamela Hansford, 15
Johnston, Mary, 9, 110, 127
Jones, Anne Goodwyn, 9
Jones, Gayle, 84
Jong, Erica, 12, 15, 63, 88
Joyce, James, 35, 36, 95, 124
Jung, Carl, 45, 46

Kaplan, Sydney Janet, 74
Kasdan, Margo, 1
Kefala, Antigone, 50
Keith, Marian, 133
Kelley, Edith Summers, 71
Keyser, Elizabeth Lennox, 75
Kingston, Maxine Hong, 5, 62
Kornfield, Eve, 76
Krause, Janet Boettcher, 118

Labovitz, Esther Kleinbord, 10, 119
Lamming, George, 120
Langland, Elizabeth, 1
Larsen, Nella, 84
Laurence, Margaret, 6, 91, 110
Lawrence, D. H., 124
Lazarre, Jean, 8, 116
Lee, Dorothy H., 28
Le Guin, Ursula K., 12
Lehmann, Rosamond, 129
LeSeur, Geta J., 77, 120
Leslie, Eliza, 2
Lessing, Doris, 1, 3, 5, 6, 10, 13, 15, 22,
    35, 42, 53, 69, 74, 87, 89, 96, 100, 103,
    107, 110, 115, 117, 119, 123, 129, 130,
    131
Lispector, Clarice, 1
Lukens, Cynthia Diane, 121
Lurie, Alison, 8, 116, 125
Lysenko, Vera, 133

Mace, Betty W., 8, 116
Mahlendorf, Ursula R., 29, 30
Mannheimer, Monica Lauritzen, 78
Mansbridge, Francis, 79
Mansfield, Katherine, 25
Marshall, Paule, 21, 77, 120
Maxwell, Ann, 46
McCullers, Carson, 4, 8, 16, 68, 114, 116,
    126, 127
McDonnell, Jane, 80, 81
McDowell, Deborah E., 82
McGowan, Marcia Phillips, 122
McIntosh, Maria, 2
McKay, Claude, 77, 120
Mecke, Mary Amanda, 123
Meredith, George, 132
Meriwether, Louise, 48
Miller, Isabel, 6, 125
Mitchell, Margaret, 9, 66
Montgomery, Lucy Maud, 76, 133
Moore, George, 27
Moretti, Franco, 11, 83
Morgan, Ellen, 31

Morrison, Toni, 5, 6, 28, 40, 84, 112, 120
Morrow, Honoré McCue Willsie, 106
Munro, Alice, 6, 86, 95, 133

Newman, Francis, 127
Nichols, Mary Sargeant, 2
Nietzke, Ann, 8, 116

Oates, Joyce Carol, 24
Olsen, Tillie, 32, 60
O'Neale, Sondra, 84
Osborne, Marianne Muse, 124

Pannill, Linda, 85, 125
Parker, Pamela Lorraine, 126
Pearson, Carol, 12
Peixoto, Marta, 1
Perrakis, Phyllis Sternberg, 86
Perry, Constance Marie, 127
Petesch, Natalie L. M., 15
Petry, Ann, 84
Phelps, Almira Hart, 2
Piercy, Marge, 26, 62
Plath, Sylvia, 8, 15, 25, 30, 35, 92, 99, 116,
    127
Plender, Martha Holman, 128
Pope, Katherine, 12
Porter, Katherine Anne, 68, 125
Pratt, Annis, 3, 14, 23, 32, 33, 87

Radcliffe, Ann, 32, 117
Reardon, Joan, 88
Rebolledo, Tey Diana, 70
Rhys, Jean, 1, 107, 117
Rich, Adrienne, 3
Richardi, Janis Marie, 129
Richardson, Dorothy Miller, 10, 15, 119,
    129
Richardson, Henry Handel, 53, 57, 64,
    123
Richler, Mordecai, 133
Rios, Isabella, 48
Rivera, Tomás, 70
Roe, Karen E., 1
Rose, Ellen Cronan, 1, 13, 89, 130
Rosenberg, Ann, 58
Rosowski, Susan J., 90
Ross, Catherine Sheldrick, 91
Rossner, Judith, 112
Rubin, Jerry, 103
Russ, Joanna, 12
Ryan, Maureen, 14

Salinger, J. D., 35
Sand, George, 18, 128
Sandbach-Dahlstrom, Catherine, 33
Sarton, May, 15, 110
Sayers, Dorothy, 5
Schreiner, Olive, 32, 87
Schvey, Henry I., 92
Schwaiger, Brigitte, 1
Secor, Cynthia, 34
Sedgwick, Ann Douglas, 127
Sedgwick, Catharine, 2, 98
Sexton, Anne, 1
Shabka, Margaret Collins, 131
Shakespeare, William, 4
Shange, Ntozake, 3
Shulman, Alix Kates, 31
Sidney, Margaret, 76
Silver, Brenda R., 1
Sinclair, May, 15, 87, 123, 129
Smedley, Agnes, 5, 90
Smith, Betty, 8, 116
Smith, Stevie, 123
Sommers, Jeffrey David, 132
Southworth, E. D. E. N., 2
Spacks, Patricia Meyer, 35
Spark, Muriel, 4, 15, 115
Stafford, Jean, 14, 16, 24, 67
Stead, Christina, 37, 127
Stead, Robert J. C., 133
Stefan, Verena, 1
Stein, Gertrude, 34
Stein, Karen F., 93
Stendahl, 103
Stephens, Ann Sophia, 2
Stephens, Harriet Marion, 2
Stewart, Grace, 15, 94
Stimpson, Catharine R., 1
Stoddard, Elizabeth Drew Barstow, 102, 104
Stouck, David, 36
Stowe, Harriet Beecher, 2
Struthers, J. B., 95
Suckow, Ruth, 16, 127
Swados, Elizabeth, 8, 116

Tennenbaum, Silvia, 8, 116
Tiger, Virginia, 96

Townsend, Virginia, 2
Turner, Gordon Philip, 133
Tuthill, Louisa C., 2
Tyler, Anne, 7

Updike, John, 7

Vincent, Sybil Korff, 97
Voloshin, Beverly R., 98

Wagner, Linda W., 99
Walker, Alice, 25, 48, 62, 82, 93, 112
Ward, Elizabeth Stuart Phelps, 8, 15, 94, 116, 127, 128
Warner, Anna, 2
Warner, Susan, 2, 98
Warner, Sylvia Townsend, 68
Washington, Mary Helen, 1
Waxman, Barbara Frey, 100, 101
Weir, Sybil, 102
Wells, H. G., 132
Wells, Susan, 103
Welty, Eudora, 63, 68, 122
Wharton, Edith, 16, 113, 114
White, Barbara Anne, 16, 32
Wiggin, Kate Douglas, 76
Wilson, Angus, 115
Wilson, Ethel, 133
Winsloe, Christa, 1
Wolfe, Christa, 10, 119
Woodbury, Helen, 127
Woolf, Virginia, 1, 5, 15, 22, 25, 31, 44, 87, 94, 111, 121, 123, 128, 131
Wright, Sarah, 77, 120

Yonge, Charlotte, 33
Young, E. H., 115

Zacharia, Lee, 41
Zagarell, Sandra A., 104
Zajdel, Melody M., 105
Zilboorg, Caroline, 106
Zimmerman, Bonnie, 1